PREFACE

I wrote this book in the early 1990s when my children were very young. They are now adults. They have amazed me countless times throughout the years by their actions and accomplishments, sometimes positively, sometimes not-so-positively. Like all humans, they are still works in progress. I should not try to take the credit unless I'm also willing to take the blame.

I put the book aside for many years before deciding to revisit it. When I read the original manuscript, I felt like I had captured a written snapshot of the life of our family during that particular time. I remembered events I had long since forgotten, and I realized that over twenty years brings changes, surprises, disappointments, and joy. In some ways, I miss my children being young, and, in other ways, I'm glad it's over.

Mostly I'm glad it's over.

In no way do I claim to be an expert on child rearing, or anything else for that matter. I have mellowed somewhat over the years, and, like almost everyone, I would change some things if I could go back. Would the new results be better? Impossible to know, and a waste of time to worry about.

While I still encourage a parent to try to stay home with his or her young children if possible, I also know that, for most families, it is necessary for both parents to work. If that is the case for you, then don't feel guilty, and try to spend as much time as you can with your children when not working.

But if either you or your spouse can work from home, or if you can juggle hours and shifts so one or both of you can be with them as much as possible, both you and your children will benefit. While the intended audience for this book is men who are stay-at-home dads, all parents will probably recognize themselves or their children somewhere in this modest tome.

Much has changed since this was originally written. Technology has changed dramatically. When first written, there was no internet, no cell phones, no DVDs. Homes still had land line telephones, and most did not have computers. Video games were fairly new, and no one imagined taking pictures or videos with a phone which was solely used for making phone calls. Whoever heard of a text message back then? And, for those too young to remember, videos were recorded on video tape and taken with a video camera and played on a VCR player.

I debated how much to update the material. My wife wanted me to leave everything as written, but I did update a few things, such as changing VHS to DVD. I didn't add references to newer technologies, mostly because there seemed to be no need. Kids are kids, even if families and technology have changed. Whether your child is watching television or watching something on the internet, he or she is still spending time absorbing whatever is being watched.

The original manuscript also made some references to outdated theories on nutrition, primarily that all fats are bad. New research led me to make some minor changes in this area. Some fats still are best avoided, and, of course all fats still contain a large number of calories, but it's good to add some healthy fats to our diets in moderation. In no way do I claim to be an expert on nutrition. Research these issues yourself, as they are important to both you and your children, and information changes. There is at least some truth in the idea that food is medicine. It can also be poison over time.

I also debated whether or not to add a chapter or two about teenagers, but decided against it. I don't think our children were typical teenagers anyway, as they waited until they were a bit older before acting like you'd expect teens to act. While I think this was a good thing, I don't dare try to take credit for it.

Like I said, if I take the credit, then I also have to take the blame.

That's something parents should always remember. No matter how hard you try, and no matter how well you do while parenting, your children have free will and minds of their own, and they will sometimes make bad decisions. You may feel you failed somehow, and you may spend countless hours beating yourself up, second-guessing yourself, wondering what you did wrong.

Stop. Sure, you made mistakes. You're human. And so are your children. They will also make mistakes. They may rebel against what you taught them. They may fall in with a bad crowd. They may just do foolish things because, well, for the same reasons you did foolish things at their ages.

Forgive yourself for any mistakes, real or imagined, and accept your children for who and what they are while always hoping and praying that they will be safe and eventually become the people they were meant to be. Unconditional love is what we all want. Loving your children unconditionally is not always easy, but it's the most important gift you can give to them.

And, maybe, just maybe, one day they will love you unconditionally, too.

Disclaimer

My wife insisted I make it known that some of the scenarios in this book are real events that actually happened while others are based on actual events that have sometimes been augmented for humor or to make a point. I think most of these latter situations are self-evident, but I wouldn't want the reader to think that every word was absolutely, precisely, and emphatically true.

Just read it, you'll figure it out.

INTRODUCTION

You've made THE DECISION. After countless hours of discussion with your wife, after sleepless nights of soul-searching and self-doubting, you and your spouse have made the decision--YOU, a big, burly, strong, macho, testicle-scratching man, have decided to stay at home with the kids while your wife ventures into the world of full-time employment.

No longer will you get your identity from your job. No longer will you be the primary breadwinner. You have taken on the awesome task of wiping noses and bottoms, of running an unpaid taxi service for the underage crowd, and of trying to get them to eat something, ANYTHING, that's not predominately sugar. From now on you will stammer and stutter whenever someone asks, "What do you do?" and pretend you don't notice the peculiar looks you get when you answer.

You will also have the satisfaction of knowing that you, and not some nameless daycare worker, will be the primary caregiver for your children. No matter how bad your cooking, or how sloppy your family room, at least you will have the satisfaction of knowing that you gave your time, your energy, your love--yourself--to your offspring, even if they won't always seem to appreciate it.

You will now be expected to nurture, to kiss boo-boos, and to referee sibling rivalry. You will be the one they call when they're hurt, scared, or angry. You will be the one they expect to solve all problems, to satisfy their every whim--immediately. Out of habit, you may be the one they call on when they wake up from a nightmare in the middle of the night, or the one they call when they need to vomit.

You will probably have to help with homework, cook meals, buy groceries, and do laundry. You most likely will find yourself sweeping and mopping, dusting and straightening, and knocking down cobwebs.

You will get endless exercise as you pick up clutter, help with baths, and change diapers, assuming your kids are still young. If they're older, then you'll be driving them everywhere, worrying where they are and who they're

with, and trying to motivate them to work hard in school and/or part-time
jobs.

But, no matter how they turn out in the end, at least you'll know you tried--
you really tried--and maybe, just maybe, they'll wipe YOUR bottom
someday.

YOU KNOW YOU'RE REALLY A PARENT WHEN...

All sorts of disgusting bodily functions no longer make you gag.

You can't imagine going anywhere without armfuls of bags, carriers, toys, bottles, clothes, and other assorted necessities.

You don't remember what it's like to sleep through an entire night uninterrupted.

Finding your necktie in the refrigerator doesn't seem particularly strange.

Your walls are noticeably dirty from the floor to a height of about three feet, and remarkably clean from there to the ceiling.

Privacy? What's that?

You are able to continue a phone conversation calmly while all hell breaks loose around you, and you are only vaguely aware of who's hitting whom.

Time for yourself? You've got to be kidding.

The idea of going anyplace with the kids, for any reason whatsoever, seems totally ludicrous.

You have never felt as much joy as when you're hugging your little one, even if that really is a dirty diaper you smell.

You can't remember what you did with all your free time before the children were born.

You realize that your own parents weren't so bad after all.

You can no longer relate to people who don't have children.

You notice all the violence and foul language on television that never bothered you before.

You hope and pray that your children don't do some of the things you did in your youth.

Something seems wrong on those rare occasions that the house is actually quiet.

You'd cut your own heart out to keep theirs from breaking.

In spite of all the chaos and confusion, you wouldn't trade your life for all the money in the world.

PARENTAL STYLES

or

Maybe Mom Knew Something About
Raising Kids After All

Not until I became a parent did I begin to understand some of my own parents' actions--and reactions. It has been said that most people parent much as they were parented, even when they believe their parents did a lousy job.

Never mind that they swore they'd NEVER say that to their children or react that way to their kids' behavior. When it comes time to do the job of parenting, and it most definitely is a job, most people fall into the only pattern they know, the pattern of parenting they learned on their parents' knees.

I was quite shocked the first time I heard my parent's voice coming from my mouth. Actually, I hear two voices. Sometimes I sound like my father, and sometimes I sound like my mother. My parents had very different parenting styles, and, as a child, I preferred my father's less disciplined, more permissive style. (Never mind that my mother had the responsibility of the vast majority of the childcare duties, both in time and hands-on care.)

As a parent, however, I understand the need for discipline, even if I don't always administer it appropriately. While I have been described as a "marshmallow," a "push-over," and, as our six-year-old occasionally referred to me, the "first maid," I still can be firm when the situation warrants firmness.

I think discipline is the hardest part of parenting. Discipline and punishment are not synonymous, but exactly how do they differ? When is one appropriate and not the other? How do you get a head-strong child to do your bidding without being a bully? Is it possible to teach children to WANT to do the right thing?

I'm much less critical of my own parents now that I have children. Like so many of their generation, my mother was the constant parent, the one who did virtually all the day-to-day chores involved with child-rearing. My father worked long hours, was often out of town on business, and, as was common in that by-gone era, my mother did all the diaper changing, dressing, feeding, etc., for the children.

She was also the housekeeper, laundress, did most of the yard work, and began working outside the home at about the time I was ten. It was definitely a man's world, and, guys, it's definitely over. It wasn't fair then, it's not fair now, and only a few relics from the past really believe their wives should wait on both them and the children, wash the clothes, cook the food, clean the house, and, usually, also bring in additional income. I think most younger people agree that the chores of married life, which obviously includes childcare, should be shared.

Still, old habits and views die hard. I consider myself to be relatively enlightened to women's issues, but I remember one chauvinistic day, soon after our wedding, when I stood by the ironing board, ironing a shirt. Even though I had occasionally been in that very position while single, I suddenly had the most wicked thought--"What's the point of being married if I still have to do my own ironing?"

I knew it was wrong the moment I thought it. I was surprised that I'd thought it, yet, there it was, sullying my brainwaves, this throwback to my grandparents' generation.

I can imagine how hard it must be for men who identify strongly with their fathers and grandfathers and haven't a clue as to how to function in today's complicated world. What is woman's work? What is man's work? Which married partner is responsible for what?

Why is it if the house, or the child, is dirty or in disarray, everyone looks disapprovingly at the mother, not the father? Why is it if the family is having financial hardship or problems, everyone looks askew at the father and not the mother? Why CAN'T a woman be responsible for earning the bulk of the income while the man is responsible for keeping the home fires burning?

Traditionally, women were tied to the home due to having ten or more breast-fed children. Today, most families only have a couple of kids. (It was surprising how much disapproval we received, even from family, when my wife and I announced that we were expecting our third child.) If women have the right to have careers outside the home, then men should have the right NOT to have careers outside the home, assuming the couple can afford for one to be a stay-at-home mom.

Er, dad.

"You want to do what?"

"I want to stay home with the kids."

"You mean today?"

"I mean every day."

"You're kidding."

"That's one way to say it."

"Why?"

"Somebody needs to."

"But that's a woman's job!"

"Fathers can't take care of their own kids?"

"No, they're men."

"What's wrong with men?"

"They're helpless when it comes to children."

"Who told you that?"

"My mother."

"Who told her?"

"My father."

BREAST-FEEDING

or

All Right, So There Really Is One Thing
A Woman Can Do Better Than You

In spite of my own inability to do it, or perhaps because of my inability to do it, I am a strong believer in the benefits of breast-feeding, which, arguably, is the biggest obstacle to Daddy trying to raise the baby. All three of our children were breast-fed for about a year and a half, even though I began being a househusband when the baby was barely one-year-old. She was partially weaned at that time, but still nursed at night, on weekends, and any other time that her mother was with her.

While it is difficult to breast-feed and work outside the home, it can be done. Perhaps baby can visit mommy one or more times during the day, maybe at lunchtime. Another possible solution is to supplement breast-feeding with bottle feeding, either using baby formula or, preferably, mother's milk that has been pumped and saved.

When our first child was a baby and my wife returned to work, she carried a small ice chest and breast pump with her to work and spent her breaks in the ladies' room making milk. The main problem with this approach is that some babies--namely our first--absolutely refuse to have anything to do with a nipple that smacks of plastic.

We tried big nipples, little nipples, funny-shaped nipples, colored nipples, nipples with big holes, nipples with small holes, nipples with no holes (pacifiers), but nothing worked. There were only two nipples she would put in her mouth, and they both belonged to her mother. And she could cry indefinitely as she waited for them to be brought to her, preferring starvation to plastic.

Fortunately, the other two children were less picky about nipples, although neither had any use for pacifiers. Once the baby is old enough to eat solid food, or at least baby food, the nipple problem becomes less critical. In the meantime, just relax as the baby howls incessantly for his mother, and remind yourself that this is just a phase, nothing more, and it will pass.

Like countless other phases still to come.

"Why is the baby doing that?"

"Oh, it's just a phase."

"That's what you said last month."

"It will pass. Remember his last phase?"

"You said it would pass, too."

"And it did."

"But now this!"

"It will also pass."

"Then what?"

"Another phase, I suppose."

"How many phases are there anyway?"

"I don't know. Lots, I think."

"Are they all as bad as this?"

"Oh, no. Some are much worse."

"I won't survive."

"You'll survive."

"He'll make me old."

"He'll keep you young."

"What difference does it make if I have to continuously
   live through all these phases?"

"They, too, shall pass."

"Then what?"

"Then you'll have grandchildren to care for."

TIME ALONE

or

Count Your Blessings If You Can Pee in Peace

As a househusband, your primary job is caring for the kids, which is most assuredly a full-time job. So, don't plan on EVER finishing anything again for the rest of your natural life.

"Daddy, I'm hungry."

"I'm busy right now. Didn't you just eat?"

"Yes, but I'm still hungry."

"All right."

"Daddy?"

"Yes, dear, what is it now?"

"I'm thirsty."

"Did you finish your juice?"

"I don't like it."

"I'll get you something else."

"Daddy?"

"I'm working right now."

"Can you hold me?"

"For just a minute."

"Daddy?"

"Now what?"

"Can you play with me?"

"As soon as I finish."

"Can I help?"

"No, sweetheart, you're too young."

"Daddy?"

"Yes?"

"My stomach hurts."

"Do you need to go to the bathroom?"

"Oh."

"Back already?"

"There's a bug in the bathroom."

"It won't hurt you."

"I think it's a black widow."

"Is it a spider?"

"Or a bee."

"I'll look in a minute, as soon as I'm done."

"Can I go outside?"

"Sure."

"Will you go with me?"

"I'll come out as soon as I've finished this."

"I'm scared."

"Just stay near your swing set; you'll be all right."

"What if there's a tornado?"

"It's not even cloudy."

"Or an earthquake."

"The safest place is outside. I'll join you in a minute.
 Just let me finish."

"Daddy?"

"What is it now?"

"Is it almost my birthday?"

At this point, you might as well put your work aside and go outside and play with your child.

I have held baby Caroline on my lap many times as I worked on this book, at times frustrated by my futile attempt to type with more than one finger. I take a deep breath and remind myself that the kids come first and that someday she will be too big to sit on my lap and slap the keys on my keyboard.

Never mind that I can't eat more than three bites of food without getting up to do something for one of the children. Never mind that I can't say more than three words on the telephone without being interrupted by some life or death problem involving who's turn it is to play with the blocks, or that having a few moments alone in the bathroom is a rare and greatly appreciated event.

Children need attention as much as adults need privacy. Someone is bound to come up short, and househusbands are notoriously unselfish, caring, and patient. We ignore, postpone, and subjugate our own needs, just as mothers have done for eons. Eating your children's leftover isn't such a bad thing, assuming you don't get too fat.

So, go ahead and give your children the attention they crave. Play with them. Talk to them. Watch cartoons with them. Draw, paint, cut, and paste with them. Take them on long walks and tell them about your childhood.

Show them rocks and flowers and clouds and bugs. Pay attention to what they have to say, and praise them for everything they try to do that's good, and be understanding when they fail. Tell them frequently that you love them, and don't pay any attention when they say they don't love you.

Because they really do, you know.

TAKING THE KIDS ALONG

or

There's a Reason They're Called "Stay-at-Home-Moms"

If I could give one bit of advice on how to take children with you when you run errands, shop, travel, etc., it would be "DON'T!"

Personally, I rather enjoy being at home with the kids, in spite of all the petty annoyances and periodic frustrations, but I really don't like to load three young children into the van and go shopping.

Even when all three are on their best behaviors, a rare even at best, dealing with cumbersome diaper bags, toys that absolutely under no circumstances can be left at home, and finding three matching pairs of socks and shoes to wear is, in a word, stressful.

Once we arrive at the store, it's usually not too bad as long as we keep moving, but check-out lines try even the most patient parent's will-to-buy.

"Can I have some candy?"

"No."

"He hit me!"

"No hitting."

"She won't let me hold my toy!"

"Let him hold his toy."

"That's not his toy! That's my toy!"

"Let him hold it anyway."

"She pinched me."

"Please behave. The line's beginning to move."

"He spit on me!"

"It'll be our turn soon."

"She's bothering me!"

"Please be patient. We're almost there."

"I didn't touch him! He's lying!"

"It won't be much longer."

"I want to go home!"

"We're getting closer."

"I have to go to the bathroom."

"I can see the register."

"Give me my toy!"

"Not much longer now."

"My stomach hurts."

"What's she doing?"

"Don't touch me!"

"She's changing the paper in the register. I can't believe
   she ran out of paper."

"Stop that!"

"How long does it take to change that stupid paper
   anyway?"

"Don't pull my hair!"

"Who needs a receipt anyway?"

"Help!!"

"Where's the manager?"

"She's hurting me!"

"Why aren't there more registers open?"

"He's kicking me!"

"Why isn't this line moving?"

"Make the baby stop crying!"

"I can cope. I can cope. I can cope..."

"Why can't I have candy? Stop hitting me! What's that
  smell? Make him stop! I want to go home!"

If taking the kids along is unavoidable, frequently remind yourself that,
although everyone in the store is staring because your two-year-old is having
a temper tantrum in the cereal aisle, all kids misbehave on occasion.
Remember, they will grow up. Really, they will.

Eventually.

Besides, it could be worse. They could be teenagers.

OVER-INDULGENCE

or

Daddy, Can I Have That Toy?
And That One? And That One?

Children want EVERYTHING they see on Saturday morning T.V. and everything related to whatever overriding interest they're going through at the moment, be it superheroes or Barbie dolls. And they absolutely must have all the other ones pictured on the back of the box.

"Can I have that?"

"Maybe for your birthday. Remind me closer to the
   time."

"Why can't I have it now?"

"It's not your birthday."

"Can I have it early?"

"No."

"Why not?"

"You have to wait for your birthday to get birthday
   presents."

"Why?"

"So you'll have something to look forward to."

"I'd rather have that toy."

Every parent knows how hard it is to say no to a child. However, unless you want to take out another mortgage on the house to keep the kid in Power Ranger accessories, you must practice saying it until it comes naturally.

"Can I have that?"

"No."

"Can I have this?"

"No."

"I want that one!"

"No."

"Can we get this?"

"No."

"I want to get that."

"No."

See? Wasn't that easy?

Being a bit of a softie, however, I do occasionally give in and agree to buy them something totally frivolous, useless, and inexpensive. I try to discuss AHEAD OF TIME what can and cannot be bought, and I always stress that, if we do buy a toy today, they must be on their best behavior and the toy must be cheap, cheap, cheap. I set a monetary limit, and I stress that we cannot go above that limit. And rest assured, they will go to the absolute maximum allowed.

Never mind that my daughter replied one day, "Well, you just spent $300 fixing the car!" to justify going over our pre-designated limit.

"The car is a necessity. That toy is not."

"Yes, it is."

"We're not going over the limit."

"I don't even like that old car."

"It's all we have."

"I'd rather have that toy."

"You wouldn't feel that way if you had to walk home."

"Yes, I would."

"What would you like instead of that toy?"

"Can I get two things?"

"Only if they're cheap."

"You never let me have anything!"

No matter what you buy them, it will never be enough. Set your limit and stick to it. If you raise it "just this time," they'll never forget, and they'll expect you to raise it next time, too.

Say what you're going to do, and do what you say.

HOUSEWORK HAPPINESS

or

Who Says You Can't Eat Off My Floor?
My Kids Do It All The Time.

Once upon a time, somewhere in the 1950s, being able to walk across a spotless kitchen floor in high-heeled shoes while cooking a monstrous steak was considered the highest attainable goal for domestic goddesses who stayed at home and rocked the cradle while darning their husbands' socks.

And then came cholesterol and the women's movement.

So, what do you, a man who NEVER wears high heels, do about that dirty kitchen floor?

When my wife and I were first married we lived in a house with a kitchen floor made of vinyl that was supposed to look like brown colored brick. The floor was rarely mopped, although when our first child was two weeks past the due date my wife was told that getting on her hands and knees and scrubbing the kitchen floor would bring on labor. She did this, but all we got was a clean floor.

Afterwards, she said she was amazed how dirty the floor was and swore that the next floor she had would show the dirt so she'd know what she was walking on.

Be careful what you wish for, you might get it.

When we moved she got her wish. Our new vinyl floor is supposed to look like white tile, with just a hint of pale gray. Every time I look at that shiny white surface, I think longingly about that ugly fake brown brick.

While the fake white tile is more attractive than the fake brown brick, every tiny little dirty spot, not to mention the huge, filthy stains, screams "MOP ME! MOP ME!" To keep it truly clean, we would have to do non-stop mopping, just as the painting never stops on the Golden Gate Bridge.

"Daddy, can I have a drink of water?"

"NO! I'm mopping the floor."

"Daddy, can I have something to eat?"

"NO! I told you I'm mopping the floor."

"Daddy, can you tell me a bedtime story?"

"I told you, I'm mopping the kitchen. Go to bed."

"It's morning, Daddy. Can we have breakfast today?"

"Can't you see I'm mopping? Go to school."

"We're home, Daddy. Aren't you through yet?"

"Would I be holding this mop if I was finished? Take a
  bath and go to bed."

"But Daddy, we're hungry!"

"Nobody comes in this kitchen until I finish mopping!"

You get the idea. I cannot say for sure that the uncleanable fake white tile vinyl kitchen floor drove my wife to get a full-time job, but I have suspicions.

It's amazing just how much dirt, food crumbs, and spilled beverages are caused by such small hands and feet. When your four-year-old spills half a box of cereal trying to fill a bowl, or your six-year-old is certain she can pour the fluorescent-dyed soft drink all by herself, remind yourself that they are learning important motor skills and really are not trying to attract roaches, ants, silverfish, moths, rats, poisonous snakes, and other assorted creatures. When your toddler tires of his lunch and throws it from the high chair to watch it fall and splatter, remind yourself that he's only trying to understand gravity and other cosmic principles.

Face it: KIDS ARE DIRTY. They attract dirt. They find dirt. They like dirt. They like to play in dirt, to roll in dirt, to really get to know dirt. After all, a three-year-old understands that to know dirt is to love
dirt.

Kids will even eat dirt, given the opportunity. Their values are not your values, and the most you can hope for is to gradually teach them to pour cereal without spilling more than a little. You may be able to get them to "wash" their hands from time to time, but don't be surprised if they balk at touching the bar of soap.

So how to clean that floor? I suggest a strong cleaner, a bucket of water, and a mop that can be abused on a weekly basis--unless of course one of you wants to bring on labor pains.

When I was a child, my mother mopped the floor once a week without fail (Mondays, I believe.) I once criticized her for doing all that "pointless" work, suggesting that the time could have been put to better use.

Then I had children of my own, and I realized that waiting an entire week between moppings meant six and a half days of dirty floor. One day of mopping each week merely keeps the dirt at a tolerable level and wards off most major third-world diseases.

It's amazing how wise your parents become once you have children of you own.

I have to confess that I hate mopping the kitchen floor--or the bathroom floor, the breakfast room floor, the front porch, and any other floor that begs to be cleaned.

> "Suffer!" I say, heartlessly ignoring the floor's need to
>   be cleaned. "Can't you see I've better things to do?"

Yeah, like sweeping, cooking, washing the thirty-third sink-full of dishes that day, and searching for the remains of last week's leftovers that are molding in the refrigerator.

> "Clean me!" the floor cries as the smudged fudge sauce stains crack and

peel.

I callously walk over the bread crumbs as my shoe smears globs of grape jelly, pretending not to notice the dried Coca-Cola stains under the chair. I try to look away from the ketchup drips and the mysterious green stuff that seems to move when I'm not looking. I cover my ears so as not to hear the incessant call of the cleanser. I look away from the mop, and, knowing the bucket is near, I try to hide in the laundry room, pretending to fold clothes.

It's no use. I sigh deeply, take the bucket bravely in hand, and walk confidently to the sink and turn on the hot water. I tell myself that mopping is good upper body exercise and, when done properly, can be an aerobic work-out. Who needs a membership to an overpriced gym, when I've got enough floors to mop to keep me fit and strong until the last child grows up and leaves home to make messes on someone else's floor. I turn on the radio, and I show that fake-marble-tile vinyl who's boss.

And when your preschooler wants to help, let him. I have an unproven theory that if you let him do something when he's too young to do it, but still thinks it's fun, he'll still want to do it when he's old enough to actually be of some help.

Mind you, it's unproven.

COMFORTING BABY

or

No, You Can't Send the Baby Back, Even If
It Does Cry and Cry and Cry and Cry...

Although we were blessed by not having what my grandmother called a "colicky baby," they really do exist, and they really do cry non-stop. Sometimes for months. Perhaps they have digestive problems, perhaps they have other physical pain, or perhaps they are just unpleasant and cranky. Nonetheless, crying babies are LOUD and difficult to contend with. You must NEVER, under any circumstances, strike the baby, scream at the baby, shake the baby or run away from home. Reasoning won't work, and it's pointless to pretend the baby isn't really crying.

So, what to do?

If you think the baby is sick, call your pediatrician for advice. There may be something seriously wrong with her that may require medical attention.

If your doctor determines that there is nothing warranting medical care, you are then on your own. Take a deep breath and let it out slowly and remind yourself that "this, too, shall pass." Try to remain calm, as some people believe that babies pick up "vibes" from those around them. Remember that the little darling isn't doing this just to annoy you or to make you or your wife late for work the next day, nor is the baby likely to be suffering from post-womb depression, even if there were such a thing.

Babies cry when they're hungry, so try to give the baby her bottle (or her mother's breast if it's available). If hunger is not causing this display of unhappiness, then check her diaper. While some babies are oblivious to a diaper full of unmentionable material, some babies are surprisingly sensitive to the least amount of dampness. Change if necessary, making certain the fit isn't too snug.

If the baby continues to cry, then rock the baby. If the crying hasn't stopped after a reasonable amount of time (this could be from fifteen to five hundred minutes, depending on your personality), try walking the baby, changing her position from time to time. As you rock or walk, if the baby has her head on your shoulder, try patting her back gently and slowly, repeatedly. You may want to try singing softly or humming, telling stories, or playing old Aretha Franklin records.

If those don't work, take the baby outside. This often will stop a crying jag. Show her interesting things, like trees and leaves and rocks. Speak softly and comfortingly. If going outside is impossible, due to weather or wild animals, or it doesn't stop the crying, then put the little darling in a baby swing, wind it up, and try not to lose your cool. You may have to wind it several times, but this always worked with our most difficult baby when she wanted something (usually her mother's breast) and had not yet learned the virtue of patience.

Just remember that the baby may be having real physical discomfort. Check for diaper rash and for clothes that may be binding or too tight. Is she too hot or cold? You may want to try giving her a bath. Our babies often felt like sleeping after a warm bath. If you have a musical toy, try winding it up. Even if it doesn't work, at least you'll have tried one more distraction.

Give her a pacifier. If she won't take it, or for some reason you don't have one, try your pinky finger. Sometimes babies want to suckle, even though they're not hungry.

If all else fails, take the baby for a ride in the car. That often worked for us.

But if the baby is fed, diapered, washed, walked, rocked, chauffeured and sung to, and cannot be distracted by books, trees, dirt, or toys, then put some cotton balls in your ears, sit in a comfortable rocker, and put the baby on your shoulder as you sing quietly and think of the latest Dow Jones numbers.

And by all means, don't hesitate to say a prayer for patience--even if you're an atheist.

SCHOOLYARD PROFANITY

or

I NEVER HEARD WORDS LIKE THAT
UNTIL I WENT TO COLLEGE

Oh, the first day your little darling comes home and curses at his little sister, saying words that would make your grandmother clutch her chest in the throes of death.

Kids learn a great deal at school, and the teacher is responsible for only a small fraction of it. We are currently in the middle of "cool." My first grader says "cool" at absolutely every opportunity.

"We're having ice cream for dessert tonight."

"Cool!"

"It's supposed to be very warm tomorrow."

"Cool!"

"Mama has to work late tonight."

"Cool!"

"Aunt Jane has the flu."

"Cool!"

"We're three months behind on the mortgage payment."

"Cool!"

"Your mother and I are separating, the dog has a
    terminal illness, the sewer line is clogged, locusts are
    taking over Rhode Island, and the end of the world will
    be in exactly ten minutes."

"Cool!"

"Cool" may or may not be an improvement over "neat" or "groovy," but it definitely grates on my nerves. If she only said it occasionally, I wouldn't mind or even notice. But EVERYTHING that isn't personally tragic, such as who is now her former best friend's new best friend, is "cool."

She doesn't say, "That's cool." I suppose that wouldn't be cool. She only says, "Cool!" Anything that is nice, good, exciting, wonderful, amusing, thrilling, heart-warming, pleasant, entertaining, mesmerizing, joyful, amazing, tantalizing, titillating, awe-inspiring, acceptable, pleasantly unusual, mystical, magical, or stupendous is, in a word, simply "cool."

Why waste words.

So what to do when Junior embarrasses the entire extended family at the family reunion by rattling off a few choice phrases that he may or may not understand, and that are considerably less acceptable in polite society than "cool"?

Is a bar of soap needed to wash out the offensive mouth, or is a "Please, Dear, don't say those nasty words" more appropriate to dissuade the offensive behavior?

The "carrot and stick" approach has long been used to stop unwanted behavior in children, with success in many instances. The "carrot" is a reward for desirable behavior, and the "stick" is punishment, not necessarily of a physical nature, for unwanted behavior. Offer a reward for stopping the gutter talk and offer a promise of punishment for using the inappropriate words.

Be sure to specify EXACTLY which words or phrases are unacceptable and try to give reasons why. If the little dear cannot or will not accept the reasons, then explain that such talk just is not acceptable in our family--end of explanation.

While I think it's important to explain the reasoning behind family rules, rules do not need to be justified or defended. They are the rules because the parents have made them the rules, and if the rules change the children will be notified in due time. Remember, PARENTS ARE IN CHARGE. Say it as often as necessary.

PARENTS ARE IN CHARGE, PARENTS ARE IN CHARGE.

Don't you feel better just saying the words? Sometimes I worry it's really the children who are in charge, but you'll never hear me say it in front of my kids, lest I undermine my power base.

Experts in child-rearing, of which I am not, insist that kids, like dogs, WANT someone, preferably one or more parents, to be in charge. I accept this as fact, and I make it a point to never discuss it with my kids, lest they convince me otherwise.

"Why do I have to do that?"

"Because it's best for you and for our family."

"Nobody else has to do that."

"If they live in this house they do."

"Then I don't want to live here either."

"Someday you will grow up and move away."

"Well, after that I'll NEVER do that again."

"You will when you have children."

"Then I'll never have children! I'll have cats instead."

"We only baby-sit children--not cats."

"You don't love me!"

"Of course we love you."

"If you loved me, then you'd love my cat!"

"But you don't have a cat."

"You hate my cat!"

"We don't hate the cat that you don't have."

"I don't believe you."

"It's true. Why, we love all the cats you don't have."

"You sure?"

"Almost as much as we love you."

"Really?"

"Really."

"Then why won't you baby-sit my cat?"

"O.K., we will. We'll baby-sit the cat you don't have
 any time you want."

"Even on Sunday?"

"Especially on Sunday."

"Do I still have to brush my teeth?"

"Everyone in this house has to brush their teeth."

"Not my cat!"

"Everyone except your cat."

"You don't make the baby brush her teeth."

"The baby doesn't have any teeth."

"My cat has teeth." (Crying) "You don't love my cat!"

To avoid such conversations, and I assure you that you do want to avoid conversations such as these, it's best to just state that teeth are to be brushed before bedtime--no exceptions, no arguments, no explanations. While you may have to be firm on occasion, most likely the routine will soon become just that--routine.

As far as language, what YOU say and how you talk is the first and most important lesson you children will learn about appropriate speech. If you curse like the proverbial sailor, why would you not expect your children to do the same? This is also true for virtually everything else in life. You teach them every minute by your actions, your words, you examples.

If you don't want them to do it, then you probably shouldn't do it either.

NO REST FOR THE WEARY

or

There'll Be Sleep Aplenty in the Grave

I'll admit it--I hate to get up early. I don't mind staying up late, and I don't mind getting up during the night (or even after the sun rises), provided that I can sleep in. I've always believed that the very best sleep occurs after the sun rises, and I strive to spend as much time as possible in bed each and every morning while those early birds are out searching for slimy worms in the cold, cold morning air. Let's face it--nothing good happens before noon, and I enjoy nothing more than lounging around in bed for half the day.

Fat chance.

I remember the carefree days of my youth when I could go to bed whenever I wanted, sleep without interruption, and arise refreshed after double digits defined the hour. Even if I couldn't do this every day, I could on occasional weekends and holidays.

Then I married and we had a child, and I haven't known an uninterrupted night's sleep since. I understand that some babies sleep through the night without waking. Mind you, I've never seen one personally, but I've heard rumors.

Still, I'm not complaining, because I've also heard about babies that cry non-stop all night long, only to fall asleep ten minutes before the alarm clock sounds. Although all of our children awoke, usually to nurse, several times throughout the night, as they got older, they awakened less often and were quicker to fall back asleep. There was still the occasional bad dream or need for help to go to the bathroom, but generally it was the baby who woke up consistently night after night for what seemed like eons but actually couldn't have been more than a couple of brief years.

"Still sorting baby clothes?"

"It's hard to believe he was ever so small."

"We could have a yard sale."

"I could never sell his things. Why, just look at these
   tiny shoes."

"We could give them to charity."

"I should save them for my sister. I'm sure she'll get
   married and have children someday."

"I thought you wanted to clean out the drawers."

"I do, but my sister may need them."

"Then let's give everything to your sister."

"Everything? I couldn't give this to my sister. She
   doesn't appreciate anything handmade."

"Then keep the booties and give her everything else."

"She wouldn't want this. She hates green."

"Then give her everything except the homemade booties
   and the green thing."

"It's not a thing, it's a jumper."

"Well, whatever it is, it'll be appreciated by some poor
   child."

"What about our poor child? The only thing he'll have
   to remember his babyhood of homemade booties."

"Oh, now, don't cry. Maybe we should keep the green
   thing, too."

"I'm not crying. I just got a piece of lint in my eye. Of
   course we'll keep the green jumper. And these overalls.
   Aren't they darling?"

"Darling."

"I couldn't part with this...or this...or these..."

"You're putting everything back!"

"How could we get rid of his first pair of long pants? Or
 his first hat? Or this shirt with the tractor on it?"

"What about your sister?"

"My sister? My sister? She won't appreciate these
   priceless memories!   How could I part with these
   shoes? Remember this jacket? He wore it on his first
   birthday. Look at this sweater. Isn't it adorable? And
   these tiny, little socks! That settles it. We're keeping it
   all."

"All of it?"

"Every mismatched sock. I don't know how I could let
   you talk me into throwing away all our precious
   memories. If you want more room you'll just have to
   buy a bigger house."

Why does the period during which you have a baby in the house seems to last
forever--until you get rid of the last diapers and put the high chair in the attic
next to the crib? Then you wonder how the time passed so quickly.

As you pack up the last of those tiny clothes and wonder if the diaper bag
would make a good bowling bag, you'll find yourself actually missing sitting
in a dark room, singing lullabies off-key as you rock an exhausted baby who
fights to stay awake.

Unless you have another baby, of course.

TRANSPORTATION

or

Forget the Sports Car,
Do They Still Make Station Wagons?

When my wife was very pregnant with our third child, we realized that our small sports-style automobile, designed for two petite adults in front and two legless torsos in back, simply wouldn't be big enough for two adults, two car seats, and one energetic kindergarten student. Although the car was paid for and still ran well, we knew we had to bite the bullet and get something bigger.

We wisely went car shopping without the kids, which was a better date than going to the grocery store, and we were feeling that rush of adrenalin that only comes when sitting in a brand-new car. I'm not certain, but I think it may come from the fumes of the new upholstery.

We sat in the front seat of the car of our choice and both turned and looked at the rather small back seat. Apparently, the same image--three children sitting in a row like sardines in a can--simultaneously flashed through both our heads. We looked at each other, shook our heads, and in unison said "no."

Then we asked to look at the used mini-vans.

When I was a child and cars were still as big as most living rooms, families even then felt a need for something bigger, namely a station wagon. It seemed that all families, even those with only the "ideal" two children, needed a station wagon. Maybe it was just a fad, like pick-up trucks and line dancing, because my fifth-grade school teacher had one, and she didn't even have any children.

I was crazy about our first, and only, station wagon. It was a monstrous blue thing with a rear seat that faced backwards, seemingly only inches from the huge rear window that went down completely into the rear hatch door. I longed to ride in back with the window down and watch where we'd been. My father, however, had other ideas.

"Daddy, can we put down the back window?"

"No."

"We won't fall out."

"No."

"Why not?"

"Fumes."

"What?"

"Fumes. I can't stand to smell the exhaust fumes."

"The what?"

"They give me a headache."

"What?"

"The exhaust fumes give me a headache."

"What fumes?"

"The fumes from the tailpipe."

"I don't smell any fumes."

"That's because the window is up."

"Well, put it down and let's see if there's any fumes."

"Don't you open that window!"

"I want to smell the fumes."

"I said not to open that window."

"There aren't any fumes."

"Close that window!"

"All I smell is fresh air. I know fresh air won't give you

a headache."

"Shut that window or I'm going to stop this car!"

"It's not a car, it's a station wagon...Don't stop! I'm
 shutting it!"

"Hurry up!"

"I'm trying! I think it's stuck!"

"Move your hands, I think I can do it from up here."

"Maybe it's broken."

"Move your hands!"

"I can't close it!"

"MOVE YOUR HANDS!"

"How'd you do that?"

"There's an electric switch."

"Electric? Where's the extension cord?"

"There is no extension cord. The car has a battery and a
 generator."

"Can we watch T.V.?"

"Of course not."

"If we can't open the window then I want   to watch
 T.V."

"You can't watch T.V. Just look out the window."

"I'd rather watch Lucy. When will we be there?"

"In about four hours."

"I can't look at that old truck for four hours."

"I'm sure it won't be behind us the entire trip."

"Can I wave?"

"Don't wave at strangers."

"I can't do anything. How much longer?"

"Four hours."

"How can it still be four hours? Can we open the
 window?"

"No!"

"I'm bored."

"Read a book."

"Will you read it to me?"

"I can't. I'm driving."

"Can we open the window?"

"NO!"

"We can't do anything. How much longer?"

"I have a headache."

"Then we might as well open the window and let the
 fumes in."

"Don't touch that window!"

"How come you have a headache if the window's
 closed? Are we there yet? I'm tired of riding
 backwards. Can we stop and get something to drink?
 I'm thirsty...I think I need to go to the bathroom...I want
 to watch T.V. Are you sure we can't put the window down?"

Ever wonder why some parents want their kids to be just like them?

PLAYING SECRETARY

or

Is Your Wife at Home?

Now that your wife is busy, busy, busy in business with all of its related business meetings, social events, and other trappings, you may find that she gets most of the phone calls. People constantly seem baffled that I am home during the day while my wife is at work.

"You must be babysitting today," they say as they hear children screaming in the background.

"Yes," you reply, as you try to stop little Debbie from hitting little Stevie in the head with a can of soup.

"You must have the day off," they say, waiting for a reply.

"Would you like me to have her call you?" you ask, preferring to avoid a lengthy discussion.

Try not to let this sort of thing damage your possibly fragile ego. So what if everyone wants to talk to your wife? So what if everyone who calls thinks you're the gardener? So what if they do think you can't get a job or that she's more important than you? So what if they think you're a lazy, no-good bum who mooches off his poor, overworked wife?

So what?

At least you have the satisfaction of knowing that little Johnny drank his milk that day and that you were there to comfort him when he fell down and bumped his chin while climbing on the coat rack and, believe it or not, that's just as important as the latest merger in corporate America.

I'm always amazed that some men consider raising children to be unimportant or "unskilled." My four-year-old's pre-school teacher recently said that I "should talk to some of these other dads "about what it's like to take care of children." I replied that if more men took care of children, then women would get more respect.

Taking care of young children is immensely rewarding, very fulfilling, at least at times, and can be extremely satisfying. However, it is definitely not easy. It is challenging to both body and spirit, and, unfortunately, it is too often unappreciated and undervalued.

Human beings are, by nature, creative beings. Our society values creativity in the arts, in business, and, whether good or bad, in politics. Surely another human being is as valuable to society as another painting or a catchy logo for a new brand of cigarettes.

To me, the absolutely most unbelievable thing my wife and I have ever done, either separately or together, was to create three brand-new human beings. No matter what I do for the rest of my life, I will never be able to surpass this feat. There are now three people in the world who did not exist before. They may do great good, or they may do great harm, but, whatever they and their possibly uncountable descendants contribute to our world, I can take at least a minimum of credit for their very existence.

Now that beats writing a best-seller any day.

Not only can I claim partial credit (or blame, as the case may be) for our children's existence, but I can also claim partial credit for how they turn out. If all behavior is caused by genetics, then I am partly responsible. If all behavior is the result of environment, then I am partly responsible. I can try blaming my wife if the behavior is
less than 100% desirable, but if I do that, then it's only fair to give her all the credit for a good report card or an act of random kindness.

Even in one-parent households, the absent parent is partly responsible for how the kid turns out, because the very absence of someone will undoubtedly have a significant effect on the child's life. There's no way to avoid it--you are constantly having some kind of effect on your children, whether you try or not, whether you're even alive or not.

It's an awesome responsibility.

"Oh, what a beautiful child!"

"Thank you."

"Who does she look like?"

"People say she looks like me."

"And so well-behaved!"

"People say we're a lot alike."

"I can see she has your eyes."

(Modestly) "Yes."

"And what a cute outfit! Did you pick it out?"

"Yes, I did."

"She's so sweet!"

"We think so."

"Does she always drool so much?"

"What?"

"She ruining that pretty dress."

"Close your mouth, Sweetheart."

"Oh, no! She's spitting up!"

"She ate too fast."

"What's that smell?"

"Oh, oh! Must be time for a new diaper."

"Why is she screaming?"

"She's tired."

"Then why doesn't she go to sleep?"

"She can't sleep when she's this tired."

"How can you stand it?"

"I guess I'm used to it."

"That's the most obnoxious child I've ever seen!"

"She just upset, that's all."

"Who did you say she looks like?"

"Everyone says she looks just like her mother."

Remember, if you don't want the blame, then don't take the credit.

AS THE WORLD TURNS

or

What Do You Mean You're Using The
Umbrella For a Boat?

I often feel that most people live in a totally artificial world. They know virtually nothing about growing food, making clothes, building shelter, or even how to find potable drinking water. Sure, they know a world of artificial currency, human-made corporations and governments, and unbridled greed and consumerism, but do they know what it feels like to plant a seed or pluck an egg from a hen's nest?

Do they hope it won't rain since they've planned a corporate round of golf, or do they pray for rain so the potatoes won't wilt and die? Although it's without scientific study, I've observed that people who live in the real world generally welcome rain within reasonable amounts, while those living in a totally artificial, human-made world relish sunshine to an absurd degree.

     WEATHER FORECASTER--"Tomorrow will be a beautiful day, sunny, with a high of 85."

I decide to water the apple tree I planted yesterday.

   "The rest of the week looks just a   beautiful, with lots of
      sunshine and highs near 90."

I decide to water the plum trees I planted last month.

   "And it looks like the weekend is shaping up to be
      gorgeous, with clear skies, plenty of sunshine, warm
      temperatures, and perfect weather for tailgating before
      the big game."

I decide to water the grape vines I planted last fall.

"The long-range forecast is for sun, sun, and more sun!
    The temperatures will be warmer than normal and
    there shouldn't be a cloud in the sky to spoil any of
    your vacation plans."

I decide to buy more hoses.

    "The national weather service is predicting an absolute
    end to rain in the foreseeable future, so all you sun-
    worshippers can get out there and tan until your skin
    rots from cancerous lesions! You'll never again worry
    about rain spoiling your picnic! No more rained out
    ballgames or having to replace those icky windshield
    wiper blades! Nothing but glorious sun, sun, sun! Throw
    away your umbrellas and those hideously ugly
    galoshes, and go outside and soak up some rays! It's
    going to be a beautiful, sunny future! Nothing but
    parades and beach parties and sun, sun, sun! Enjoy this
    warm and sunny world, where none of you plans are
    ever spoiled by that nasty rain, even if it will be short-
    lived."

I decide to change channels.

I once heard someplace that human life. and all of corporate America, would
be impossible without a few inches of topsoil and the fact that it rains.

If there were no grocery stores, no restaurants, no frozen dinners in the
freezer and no canned food in the cupboard, could you feed yourself and your
family? If you were forced to depend only on yourself and nature, could you
even survive, let alone thrive and prosper? I wish I could claim that I could
grow plenty of food for my family, but, based on my past gardening failures,
we'd be among the first to starve.

Nevertheless, I continue to plant at least a tiny patch of something every
year. One year we harvested single-serving sized watermelons and miniature
potatoes, but at least I had some satisfaction knowing that we grew them
without the use of chemical fertilizers or pesticides.

Next time I may reconsider the organic approach.

Gardening is a wonderful hobby to expose to children, who may, at least initially, be eager to help. In theory, gardening is one of those activities that can be "enjoyed" by the whole family. The art of growing, harvesting, cooking, and eating food is as old as humankind.

Children sometimes will eat foods they claim to hate if they have a hand in it's cultivation, especially if they also help with the preparation of the hated food.

Gardening also teaches knowledge and skills both you and the children will value your entire lives. For example, I taught my oldest daughter a new skill--how to squish potato beetles with her bare hands--and my son had a ball digging in the dirt as he searched for potato tubers no bigger than marbles. I also learned something--that I should have used composted leaves or manure or something resembling fertilizer to improve the soil.

I also learned that farmers are amazing people.

Obviously, all househusbands won't be able to raise enough food to sustain their families, but if you have a patch of dirt, or even a couple of empty flower pots, and you're so inclined, plant a few vegetables. Start small, with just a few plants, and gradually work yourself up to planting the entire lower forty. And, I suggest you try do it as organically as possible because any other way really does poison planet and, ultimately, ourselves. There are numerous books and magazines to help teach you how to make compost out of all those much-maligned fallen leaves your anal-retentive neighbors neurotically rake and discard every autumn. Put them to good use.

Why stop with vegetables? If you have room, add some fruit trees, preferably varieties that can survive without spraying--a difficult feat. I've recently ordered some antique varieties of apple trees that are out of general cultivation. I've had terrible luck with a number of the more commonly grown varieties, and I hope the older cultivars will prove to be more rugged. I prefer to grow trees that will be here for my grandchildren to enjoy, even if I'm not here to fuss over them. If the trees can't survive and, hopefully, bear fruit, without constant attention and gallons of poisonous sprays, then I'd rather not grow them.

"No spray? You have to spray apple trees!"

"Why?"

"Because they are extremely susceptible to damage from
 diseases and insects. We wouldn't have all those
 perfect apples in the supermarket without spraying
 repeatedly with chemical sprays and other poisons."

"Why do they have to be so perfect?"

"What! You'd eat an apple with a blemish?"
"I could eat around it."

"What if an insect bit it?"

"How much could it eat?"

"You'd actually eat an apple that was bitten by an
  insect?"

"I could eat around it."

"What kind of pervert are you?"

"An organic one?"

"You obviously don't care what kind of crud you put
  into your body. Give me clean, man-made poisonous
  residues any day! I don't care if I die of cancer or if the
  water my kids drink is full of toxic chemicals! At least
  I know that no bug came near anything I ever ate
  without dying, and that my lips have never touched an
  apple blemish. Besides, nobody has ever proven
  beyond a doubt that toxic poisons in our food water,
  soil, and air ever hurt anybody. You must be some
  kind of communist. Furthermore, everybody has to die
  of something, so it might as well be from cancer as
  anything else. Why do you want to live to be so old
  anyway?"

 "Something to do."

"Maybe you should take up golf instead."

And remember, you've not tasted potatoes until you've tasted new potatoes you grew yourself--they taste nothing like the ones you get at the grocery store.

PART-TIME WORK

or

I Just Gotta Do Something to Bring in Money

"I see from your resume, Mr. Smith, that your last job
  ended nearly three years ago. Is that correct?"

"Yes, it is."

"Then you've been unemployed since then?"

"Well, I've been working at home."

"Oh, you've been self-employed?"

"Well, not exactly."

"Have you been unemployed?"

"Well, not exactly."

"What exactly have you been doing?"

"I've been a housewife...I mean househusband."

"A what?"

Don't let it bother you. Just explain as patiently as possible. If your
interviewer is a woman, chances are, she'll respect you all the more. And if
your interviewer is a man and he seems totally bewildered and baffled, then
at least you know that you may have opened his closed mind to new
possibilities.

If you decide you need to work, then type up a new résumé and start job
hunting. Maybe it's the extra money, maybe it's self-respect, maybe it's
conditioning. But whatever the reason, if you feel a need to work, then try to
do it with the least amount of stress on the family unit as possible. It is
possible to be the primary caregiver for your children and to also bring in

income. After all, lots of women do it.

If all of your kids are in school, maybe you should consider part-time work that is flexible enough to let you play taxi driver and still let you be with the kids after school. Look upon this as an opportunity to do something interesting, something you'd never even consider as a career choice.

Although you may be working in part for the money, obviously your income will pale compared to you wife's. Don't worry about it. You're not trying to compete or compare. This is the opportunity for you to do something outrageous, experimental, unusual, or even interestingly mundane. But try to look at it as a learning experience, a chance to grow spiritually and mentally.

So what if you've never been a waiter? The tips can be lucrative and you'd be surprised how challenging it is to keep up with seven orders at once. Someone famous (Karl Marx, perhaps?) once said that everyone should change jobs every six months. Now, I'm far from a Marxist, but househusbands are in a position to do just that.

So what if the job is seasonal (maybe you can wrap Christmas packages better than anyone ever guessed) or "beneath your dignity?" I personally think that no honest work is beneath anyone's dignity. (Can't you just picture Queen Elizabeth going door-to-door selling Avon?)

Don't be embarrassed, be proud! You're working for your family, you're working for yourself. You're NOT working for the nosey neighbor down the street, unless, of course, your nosey neighbor happens to be your boss.

If you're brave enough to throw convention to the wind and be a househusband in the first place, then other people's opinions of your job choice should make little difference to you. If it's not immoral or illegal, then it's a perfectly respectable job. If you don't mind doing it, then others shouldn't mind, either. Besides, it's probably only temporary.

"What does your daddy do?"

"He used to stay home and do nothing, but now he sells
  brooms and brushes."

"Your dad sells brooms?"

"Only right now. Soon he'll be delivering pizzas."

"Can't he find a real job?"

"Oh, he has a real job. He takes care of us."

"What?"

"He cooks and cleans and drives me to dance and cans
 tomatoes from the garden..."

"What does your mother do?"

"She's a lawyer."

"Your mother's a lawyer and your daddy cans
 tomatoes?"

"Only when they're in season."

Dare to be different.

KEEPING THE LITTLE ONE HAPPY

or

Even If She Is Bigger Than You,
I'm Talking About Your Wife, Not Your Kid

It's the little things that make a person happy. The big things add excitement, but it's the little things that keep a relationship strong, and it's small things that often make or break a marriage. Try to analyze what it is that really bugs your wife and then try to make it better.

For example, my wife love paths. I'm not referring to outdoor walkways or sidewalks or moss-covered walks through the woods. I'm talking about paths through the family room, the bedroom, etc. I've discovered that keeping obvious pathways clear of debris, be it children's toys, shoes, or last week's newspapers, makes my wife happy.

She worries, perhaps needlessly, about tripping over clutter. I tell her that it will make her graceful, like a gazelle jumping over plastic Batman figures and Polly Pockets.

She is not convinced.

So, guys, quit rebelling and JUST DO IT! You'd be amazed how much cleaning and rearranging you can do in JUST TEN MINUTES. That's right, TEN MINUTES. So if you do slack off one day and watch that ballgame or soap opera instead of cleaning up the house, then the least you can do, and it is indeed the absolute least, is to get off your lazy rump ten minutes before she walks in the door and clean like crazy. To be really safe, do it before the game in case it takes eleven or twelve minutes.

Then, after you've made a dent in the dirt, go ahead and complain about how bad the kids were, how busy you were helping little Kathy with her homework, or whatever other excuses you use-- but at least do a minimum amount to keep the breadwinner happy.

"I'm sorry the house is such a mess."

"That's O.K., I'll find a chair someplace under here."

"I told Jerry not to leave all his clothes in the kitchen."

"What's this?"

"Giant fur ball?"

"Did you have a hard day?"

"You wouldn't believe. I didn't have time to cook. How about a can of beans?"

"Can I at least have a bowl?"

"Of course! You want a spoon, too?"

"I'd hoped you would have had time to wash the breakfast dishes."

"I meant to, but I couldn't find them."

"I think that's them in the corner, next to the dirty laundry."

"That's clean laundry. The dirty laundry is behind the sofa, next to the clean dishes."

"Why are the clean dishes behind the sofa?"

"Don't ask. How was your day?"

"Tiring. Is there anything to drink?"

"There's some flat soda in the sink."

"I'll just get some water. Are there any glasses?"

"Not since lunchtime, when Amy dropped them all."

"She broke all the glasses?"

"There were only three left. Just lean over and put your mouth under the faucet."

"I think I'll take a bath."

"Don't go in there unless you want a divorce."

"What's in the bathroom?"

"You don't want to know."

"Can I go in the bedroom?"

"Hold your nose if you do."

"Were the children difficult today?"

"Don't ask. Would you like some ice cream?   I just
threw the carton in the trash. There was a little stuck in
the corners. I don't melted yet."

And while she may tell you that it's perfectly O.K. not to cook dinner, try to
feed her at least three or four times a week. You'd be amazed how
impressive a few leftovers can be when combined with the proper canned
vegetables. After all, she did work all day (just as you did at home), but she'd
love to relax for a few minutes with a hot meal when she gets home.

So try to feed her if at all possible. Sending out for Chinese is O.K.
occasionally, but if you really want to win her heart, you have to at least open
a few cans or take the frozen T.V. dinners off their microwavable plates and
put them on something that resembles real china.

And guys, don't worry about the additional dishes. Plates are the easiest
dishes of all to wash, followed by bowls, flatware, and glasses. It's the pots
and pans that I wish were made of paper or plastic.

Speaking of which, if you can keep the dirty dishes washed your mate will
overlook at lot of imperfection. It's not so difficult if you keep the sink filled
with soapy water and wash as you go. Mess up a plate while making the
burgers, then immediately toss it into the sink, wipe quickly, rinse, and let dry
in the rack. (Drying dishes has to be the biggest waste of time after folding
underwear.)

Mess up a spoon, dip, wipe, rinse, and let dry. Same for glasses, ice cream scoopers, and empty jam jars. Dip, wipe, and rinse. It doesn't take but a few seconds if you do it as you go. By the time you've finished cooking dinner, the only dirty dishes will be the ones holding the food and the as-yet-unused ones that may or may not be set on the table. (But a pretty table, heck, even a mediocre table that shows a minimum of effort, will pay big dividends later.)

"It's so good to be home...you cooked!"

Actually, you took last night's leftovers, drowned them in tomato sauce and onions and let them simmer for a while.

"And you mopped the floor!"

Actually, you let the kids have a water pistol fight in the kitchen and then wiped the whole mess up with a pile of dirty towels.

"You even set the table."

Actually, you did.

"Flowers, too?"

They're just some bulbs that were growing in the yard.

"I love you!"

Minimum effort, maximum pay-off.

And remember, while it may seem like sexist nonsense, my unscientific observations indicate that most women are suckers for pretty things, particularly small, delicate, and romantic pretty things. While this may not be true for all women, it can't hurt to try sticking something that's small, delicate and pretty on the dinner table, particularly if you left her favorite nightgown in the dryer too long and it melted.

You might want to pick a few flowers from the yard (remember that flowering trees are good sources, too) and stick them in a bud vase or buy some ridiculous little do-dad from the local convenience store and put it next to her plate with a sweet, heart-felt note. Even a small piece of candy pilfered from the kids and wrapped romantically will brighten her day--and yours, too.

Remember, it's the little things.

SHOULD YOU HAVE COFFEE
WITH THE GIRLS?

or

**Really, It's Not What You Think--
We Really Are Just Friends**

One of the oddest things about being a househusband is that you tend to end up seeing and talking to women who, like you, are taking care of kids, buying groceries, dealing with school administrators and teachers, taxiing kids to doctors and dentists, etc. Naturally, conversations occur. After all, you have something in common--usually, the kids.

So what to do about jealous spouses, hers or yours? Assuming everything is on the up and up, and there is no hanky-panky involved, and you're playing with fire if there is, I think the best advice would be not to be TOO chummy. Keep conversations reasonably short, try not to be alone for extended periods of time, and, above all else, avoid bodily contact.

Even if you (or she) is a "toucher," use restraint and don't hug, kiss, squeeze, give back rubs, or otherwise engage in activities that might be construed as questionable. Even if her feet do hurt, and sex is the last thing on your mind, it's still better not to rub them for her. While it's silly to constantly worry about what the neighbors will think, nonetheless, your family has to live in the neighborhood, so you want the appearance of propriety.

And if you do have an occasional cup of coffee or tea, don't, I repeat, don't, spike it. Alcohol has been known to turn an innocent situation into a scandalous one.

"What were you doing at that woman's house?"

"She just wanted my recipe for pound cake."

"You don't know how to make pound cake!"

"Yes, I do."

"You've never made a pound cake for me."

"I didn't know you liked pound cake."

"I love pound cake!"

"I'll make one for you tomorrow."

"You want me to get fat."

"No, I don't."

"Then why do you make me eat pound cake?"

"I don't make you eat pound cake."

"What else did you talk about?"

"Nothing much. The kids, stuff like that."

"Did you tell her I love pound cake?"

"No."

"Why not?"

"I didn't know you liked it."

"You know more about her than you do me."

"No, I don't."

"Does she like pound cake?"

"I guess, she wanted the recipe."

"You love her more than me!"

"I don't love her at all."

"Oh, so you just want to eat her pound cake, is that it?"

"She doesn't have any pound cake."

"A likely story!"

"She didn't even have a recipe until today."

"Ah hah!"

"It's only a recipe! It doesn't mean a thing."

"Tell that to my lawyer!"

It's probably wiser to trade recipes with another househusband, but, unfortunately, we are far and few between. If you do get chummy with one or more housewives, always remember your marriage vows, and if either spouse seems to be jealous, or if you're even the least bit tempted or you suspect that the housewife is, then cool it immediately. Infatuations generally don't last very long, so just do the right thing and, most likely, the intense feelings will soon pass.

Remember, you don't have to do everything you want to do.

WHAT TO SAY TO OTHERS

or

Does Your Daddy Work At Night?

My first grader once asked me if I went to work after everyone went to bed. She was perplexed because someone at her school (a teacher, even) commented to her that her daddy must work at night.

"What did you say?" I asked.

"Nothing," she replied. "I didn't know. I thought maybe you went to work at midnight, after everyone goes to bed."

"When did you think I sleep?" I asked.

"I don't know," she said, truly confused.

She honestly thought that I might be sneaking out late at night after she went to bed and had a secret job that she knew nothing about.

One would think I was a gigolo or something comparable.

I told my first-grader to tell anyone who asks that I work at home, which all househusbands do, whether they get paid or not. She could have said that I mop the floor (occasionally), wash clothes (often), clean bathrooms (sometimes), wash dishes (frequently), and take care of children (constantly). She could have told them that I entertain toddlers while attempting to buy groceries, run a taxi service for kids, and oversee a homework tutoring service for children who would rather have stomach flu than study. She could have told them how we vacuum so often that we've stopped putting the vacuum cleaner away, finding it simpler to tell guests that it's a piece of modern art.

She could have mentioned that I'm developing strong stomach muscles from bending over to pick up things, and that I'm losing my hearing from listening to children scream incessantly, whether fighting or playing. She neglected to say that I'll probably never sleep through an entire night again, after years of being awakened repeatedly by one or more children for reasons ranging from nightmares and night-time accidents to seemingly life-threatening needs for sips of water and parental reassurance.

She didn't mention that I check the garbage to make certain that the toddler hasn't thrown away my wrist-watch again, or that I have dreams about Barney eating Big Bird while Lambchop plays the violin and Mr. Rogers sings off-key.
In my case, I have part-time, income-producing work that I do at home, but I'm sure many stay-at-home dads are strictly "domestic gods."

"Your daddy doesn't work?"

"I don't think so."

"Why not?"

"I don't know."

"Is he handicapped?"

"I don't think so."

"Is he between jobs?"

"I don't know."

"Is he a bum?"

"I don't think so."

"Your poor mother."

"She likes him."

"How sad."

"He's not so bad."

"You're very loyal."

"Thank you."

Let's say it and say it loudly: THERE IS NOTHING WRONG WITH
STAYING HOME AND RAISING YOUR CHILDREN!!

Not only is there nothing wrong with it, but I believe it to be noble,
honorable, and probably one of the most important, if not THE most
important, job a person can have. I think it's very peculiar that our society
considers child-rearing to be unimportant and unfulfilling. Certainly it's
trying at times. Certainly it can be difficult and the rewards are mostly
intrinsic. But I think it's a sick society that looks down on people who choose
to be with their children, who choose to offer day-to-day care, guidance, and
love to the next generation.

"And what do you do?"

"I'm a full-time parent."

"But what do you do?"

"I take care of my children."

"Is that all you do?"

"No, but it's probably the most important   thing."

"You're joking."

"No."

"You just sit at home with a bunch of snot-nosed
    children all day?"

"You don't like children, do you?"

"Not especially."

"They're really quite special."

"I wouldn't know. I have a career."

"So do I."

"I thought you took care of kids."

"I do."

"I contribute to society."

"So do I."

"I will be remembered after I'm gone."

"So will I."

"I'm very important, you know."

"So am I."

"I have done great things."

"So have I."

"If you say so."

"I do."

"You're missing so much, you know."

"Yes, as are you."

"But at least I will have a good pension when I'm old.
 All you'll have is a bunch of snot-nosed grandchildren."

"I hope so."

While I understand that not all humans are cut out to be full-time parents, and that others, due to reasons often beyond their control (usually financial), are unable to be full-time parents, I honestly believe all parents should at least make an effort to raise their own children, if at all possible.

Daycare is not cheap, and there are always added expenses, such as clothes and transportation, when working. Many couples might find that they really can afford to live on one salary, if even for only a few years while their children are young, if they refocus their priorities. Maybe they would have to cut back expenses by eating out less often, or maybe they'd have to drive the old car for another year or two, but think how much it will mean to the children to know that they were loved so much that their parents curtailed their own ambitions a little for them.

This doesn't mean reminding them constantly how much you sacrificed for them or how much you suffered because of them. Martyrdom is very unattractive.

"I could have been rich and famous."

"We know."

"I gave it all up for you children."

"We know. Thank you."

"You didn't even appreciate my sacrifices."

"We're sorry."

"Doesn't matter; I'm old now."

"You're not so old."

"Too old to be rich and famous. I did it for you, you
   know."

"We know. We've heard. We appreciate it."

"You don't care."

"We care."

"I gave it up for you."

"Thank you."

"I didn't have to."

"We know."

"I wanted to. But you don't care."

"We care."

"Doesn't matter now. What's done is done. I'll never
  mention it again."

"Thank you."

"Nobody cares anyway."

"Yes, we do."

"I don't want to talk about it."

"O.K."

"What's done is done."

"That's true."

"I did what I thought was best. I sacrificed my life for
  you children and you don't even appreciate it. Doesn't
  matter. I could have been famous, you know."

"We know."

"Then stop talking about it. Are you just   trying to do,
  make me feel bad? What's done is done..."

If you don't want to do it, then don't do it.

You don't necessarily have to give up that big house on the golf course or the
dream vacation; think in terms of postponement. Unless you have many
children, you really won't spend so many years of your life child-rearing,
particularly if you stay at home only during those few years before they begin
school. Most people only have a couple of kids. It's sad they spend more
time going to college than they do with their children.

And what if you never do achieve all the things you dreamed of achieving?
Welcome to reality. Few people do. And what if your kids grow up to be
horrible adults with no morals, who despise you and everything you tried to
teach them?

Well, take comfort in the fact that you tried, even if the results were less than
perfect. You will still have the satisfaction of knowing that you honestly did

what you thought was right, and you did it the best way you knew how.

You will never wonder if things would have turned out differently if you'd been around more, and you won't have to wonder what awful things may have occurred in the daycare center.

Besides, after you're dead, they'll probably decide that you weren't such a bad guy after all.

Maybe.

THE JOY OF STAYING AT HOME

or

Do You Feel Like a Prisoner in the House?

My mother-in-law asked my wife if I felt like a prisoner. Quite honestly, I don't. I can understand how someone could feel trapped, but I never have.

Really, I haven't.

There are several reasons for this. First of all, I like our home. It's large enough not to feel cramped, yet it's not so large as to feel totally unmanageable. The house is nearly a hundred years old, and, as a confirmed old-house-lover, I find it quite pleasant, even joyful, to just be in our home.

However, and there always seems to be a however, I have to confess that, on occasion, I have imagined being in this large-but-not-too-large old house ALL BY MYSELF. And loving every second of it.

While I cannot imagine a life without a busy, loving family, and have never known as much absolute joy as I have with my children, I still occasionally long for a moment of quiet solitude--a respite from constantly caring for others, a chance to wickedly indulge myself by watching an entire movie on without stopping to tend to the kids or eating a leisurely, uninterrupted meal. I want to lavish all that attention on myself--without guilt and without paying a babysitter.

"What have you been doing all day?"

"Nothing. Absolutely nothing."

"Nothing?"

"Nothing at all."

"Were you in a coma?"

"Not at all."

"Then how can you do nothing?"

"I just relax, and nothing happens."

"How can you relax if nothing is happening?"

"That's the only way I can relax."

"Weren't you worried that something would happen?"

"I didn't think about that."

"What did you think about?"

"Nothing."

"You must have thought about something."

"I might have, but I've forgotten."

"Ah hah! You were doing something, but you just don't
   remember!"

"I don't think so."

"I bet you were very busy doing all kinds of things, but
 you just can't remember. Isn't that so?"

"No, I can remember doing nothing very clearly."

"Oh yeah? Then why can't you remember what you've
   forgotten?"

"I don't know how to answer that."

"Not surprising, considering your short-term memory."

"There's nothing wrong with my short-term memory."

"Then why can't you remember what you were doing
   when you were doing nothing?"

"Because there's nothing to remember about doing
 nothing."

"How would you know? You can't remember anything
about nothing."

"I can remember everything about nothing. Just ask
me!"

"O.K. What have you been doing?"

"I told you. Nothing."

"I rest my case."

Dreams of solitude and nothingness notwithstanding, what can a harried househusband do to feel nurtured? One suggestion is to find someone to take care of the kids one afternoon, and just do whatever you want. Don't run errands or mow grass or wash clothes. Indulge yourself. Pamper yourself. So what if you are a man? So what if you have hair on your back? You, too, need peace, quiet, and selfish self-indulgence. You're worth it, you need it, you are allowed to have it.

At least on your birthday.

I also think it helps to find a creative outlet, preferably one you can do at home. For me, writing is perfect for this. While it's nearly impossible to find a quiet time to write, I've found it's possible to find a few (sometimes VERY few) minutes here and there that are usable, even if they're not quiet. Late at night works best for me, but I
manage to steal a minute or two here and there during the day.

Well, at least sometimes.

If the kids will sit still for ten minutes watching a cartoon, then spend that ten minutes doing your own thing. But remember--DON'T GET FRUSTRATED OR ANGRY WHEN THEY INTERRUPT.

And they will ALWAYS interrupt. Expect it. Plan on it. Count on it. Don't let it bother you. Don't let it get under your skin. So what if you were in the middle of the most brilliant piece of prose ever uttered? So what if you'll never, ever have that thought again, and it could have saved the world from certain destruction? Remember, above all else, YOU ARE A

HOUSEHUSBAND. This means you are not self-centered, vain, or motivated by self-interest.

Your primary purpose for living is to take care of the household, which usually translates into wiping dirty bottoms and cleaning up, but never crying over, spilt milk. Remind yourself that you will have time for yourself again. Someday. When they're older.

If you don't die first.

SHOPPING WITH THE KIDS

or

What Do You Mean It Doesn't Fit?
That's the Size He Wore Last Year!

Face it--kids grow. Not always at the same rate, but, eventually, they grow. This means that clothes, which do not grow (although the ones marked 'Dry Clean Only" have been known to shrink when you don't), will no longer fit. Naturally, this means that all those sizes that are never accurate anyway, are now totally meaningless.

"That's a four. Why doesn't it fit?"

"That's a four 'T'."

"What's a four 'T'?"

"It's bigger than a four."

"Is it a five?"
"No."

"Is it a four-and-a-half?"

"No. It's a 'T'. Like in "toddler."

"He's not a toddler."

"No, and he's not a four 'T' either."

"Why not?"

"He's not built like a 'T'. He's too tall."

"Toddlers can't be tall?"

"They also wear diapers."

"Not when they're four."

"It's kind of like "misses" sizes for women."

"Are you a "misses"?"

"Certainly not."

"You're married."

"Yes, but you don't have to be married to be a "misses.""

"Of course you do."

"Not when it comes to clothes."

"Is that why he doesn't have to be a toddler to be 'T'?"

"Exactly."

"I'm confused."

"Don't worry about it. Just don't buy any more 'T's'."

"Or "misses.'"

"You're catching on."

"Maybe we could just hem up some of my old pants
 until he's old enough to shop alone."

"Maybe."

So what to do? Take the kids with you and let them try everything on? This may be feasible if you have a limited number of children. Generally speaking, this means one. You may also choose to take them along if the kids are "older." This usually means they're in graduate school. All other scenarios are, at best, difficult.

Then there are other, unavoidable shopping excursions, namely buying gifts for the woman who gave birth to the little darlings. There is no reason on earth, not even the fact that the gift is supposed to be from the kids, to take the children with you.

"How long can it take?" you ask yourself, as you foolishly load up the van and head for the mall. You already know what you plan to buy, you think to yourself. You know how much you're going to spend, and you only plan to go to one store. What could go wrong?

If this book could play music, the melody to *BEAUTIFUL DREAMER* would begin here.

I once took all three of my pre-school children shopping for a dress as a gift to my wife. As the gift was in honor of Mother's Day, it only seemed appropriate that we shop as a family.

Next Mother's Day, I'll just gnaw on ground glass instead.

I tried to hold the toddler while I browsed through the sales racks, the only racks that carry truly fine clothing. My five-year-old was intrigued with picking out a dress herself and only left my sight every fifteen seconds or so. The middle child, however--the ever-moving, always bouncing, three-year-old--absolutely, positively was totally incapable
of standing or sitting still. I didn't panic until I took my eyes off of him long enough to read a price tag and turned around to find him missing.

I ran to the left. I ran to the right. I looked down the aisles. I looked behind the racks. I was ready to frantically call the manager when I found him two feet from where I was originally standing--hiding in the middle of a round rack of women's dresses. He seemed oblivious to my panic and was enjoying wiping his face with a silk skirt.

I asked him, as calmly as possible, what he was doing among all the petites. He said he was "hiding." I asked why he didn't come out when I called him, and he said he was "hiding." I asked him why he was hiding when we were supposed to be shopping for a dress for Mama, but he was at a loss for an answer. To hide successfully is its own reward.

Meanwhile his older sister, who only reluctantly agreed to help look for the "hider," had found a beaded, sequined, embroidered, and ridiculously over-priced dress that would not be appropriate for any function, public or private, that's ever been held in our town. She was certain that Mom would love it as much as she did and insisted that this be HER gift to her mother, even if Daddy did pay for it.

Never mind that it cost enough to make a serious dent in the national debt or that my wife had not been that size since her twelfth birthday. This was the gift she wanted to buy for Mother's Day.

I held up a sensible blue wash-and-wear that was not only perfect for work, but was also 50% off, and suggested that Mom would like this one better. My daughter looked at me like I had suggested we set fire to her favorite doll.

"It's so...plain!" she said, a look of absolute horror in her eyes.

"Mama likes plain dresses, especially for 		work."

"But it's so ugly! It's not even pink."

"Neither is yours," I said smugly.

"But it's shiny and pretty and there's pink in the middle
 of these flowers," she said as she pointed to the garish pink and purple peonies.

I would have answered, but I had to run to Lingerie to stop the three-year-old from looking under a mannequin's underwear.

If it were not for my resolve and expertise in parenting, not to mention the promise of ice cream and a vague promise of "maybe next year," we would not have been able to leave the store with only the simple blue dress, one pair of inexpensive earrings for my wife and another for my five-year-old, and a pair of panties for Mom exactly like the pair on the mannequin.

The moral to this story: SHOP ALONE, SHOP ALONE, SHOP ALONE-- unless you absolutely have to take them with you to be certain that it fits. And then, if at all humanly possible, take only the child that needs the clothes, unless you want to buy something for all.

If you're on a tight budget, this is particularly important. For, no matter how much resolve you leave home with, you will absolutely spend twice as much if you bring along one additional child and four times as much if you bring along two. I don't know what happens after that, but I presume it involves taking out a second mortgage on the house.

Remember, if God had wanted children to shop, He would have given them credit cards.

THE JOY OF TOYS

or

I Don't Care If He Did Bite You, You Still
Can't Throw Your Brother's Batman In the Toilet

Children love new toys--particularly new toys that belong to another child. We have always tried, perhaps foolishly, to encourage sharing among our children. Although toys and other possessions may have been given to one of the children, we'd dreamed of an idyllic home in which all children played with all toys, sharing joyously.

Get real.

> "He's got my Happy Meal toy!"
>
> "Ahhhhhhh!!! She hit me!"
>
> "He spit on me first!"
>
> "Ahhhhh!!! She pinched me!"
>
> "He kicked me first!"
>
> "Ahhhhh!!! She pushed me!"
>
> "He made fun of me first!"

You get the idea. So how do you encourage the little darlings to share without remorse, to value relationships above possessions?

As clichéd as it is, children really do learn by example. If you are generous with your possessions, then they MAY do likewise, even if the seeds you plant now don't take root until the little darlings are nearing middle age and have selfish little darlings of their own to referee.

So how to get them to share until that distant time in the future? We've tried all sorts of schemes, with varying success. Here are just a few:

    1. Taking turns--It's old as dirt, they'll sulk and complain, but putting a time limit on the toy will usually keep the household from full-fledged warfare. If the children are young, be sure to keep the time short, maybe only five (or even fewer) minutes. You may or may not want to set some kind of timer to signal when time is up.

The main problem is deciding who gets the first turn. I have even gone so far as to let the person having the second turn have an extra minute or so, but this hasn't proven to be the best strategy. Coin flipping usually causes someone to cry, and using age, beginning with either the youngest or the oldest, is generally overused. You could try taking turns as to who goes first when taking turns, but it's difficult to keep track unless you consistently write it down. Try several approaches and see which works best with your kids.

    2. Who had it first?--They'll probably disagree, because the other was certain to have been playing with the stupid toy last night or last week or last year during the big blizzard. Trying to determine right of possession in this manner can also be used in conjunction with Step 1, not that it's any more successful there.

    3. Rewards and/or threats--These are two sides of the same coin, and may or may not be successful for you. If either is strong enough, you may find instant success, which could translate into NEITHER wanting to play with the toy. Still, I have found some peace by promising delightful rewards (or at least a stick of gum) for sharing and horrific punishment, such as the loss of that particular toy for any period of time ranging from a few minutes to all of eternity plus ten years, if they fail to take turns or share or whatever.

The biggest problem with promises of rewards and/or punishment is that, once promised, they must be delivered or they will become ineffective in changing behavior. So be careful what you say in anger or desperation. And if you do find that you spoke too hastily and wish to renege, explain that you will make an exception "this time" or let hem earn a lighter punishment, for example, by doing a particular task or chore. While it may slightly weaken your position, that's a better alternative than feeling forced to carry out excessive punishment simply because you spoke hastily in a moment of anger.

I have been known to threaten to take away the toy unless they work out a way to share. Although this has worked on occasion, it has also led to one or more children running from the room, crying "You don't love me!"

Remember, they learn more from what you do than from what you say. If you want them to learn sharing, or, for that matter, any other behavior, then model the behavior for them. If you share joyously, they probably will, also.

Someday.

Doting Dads

or

My Kid's Bigger, Better, Faster, Smarter, And Better-Looking, Too.

I know you want to do it. I know you think you have every right to do it. I know that your child is the best-looking, smartest, strongest, fastest, best-behaved, most advanced, wittiest, kindest, best over-all child that has ever lived or will ever live. It's only natural, considering the child's parentage.

However, when tempted, try to refrain from telling the entire world that there's not a sperm in their scrotums or an egg in their ovaries capable of producing such a gem of genetic material as this particular child. Be modest. Only brag when another insufferable braggart has laid it on thick and heavy.

Maybe your child did make the dean's list while winning absolutely all of the trophies AND the Pulitzer Prize at age seven, but remember, it's only marginally better to brag about one's offspring than to brag about oneself. Look down and smile demurely as the newspaper clipping falls from your pocket. Protest weakly as the other person picks it up and notices your child's name, picture, etc. Feign humility as you drop one of two of the details, hoping to be asked for more information.

"You dropped this. Is this little Amy?"

"Yes, it is."

"What a beautiful child. She won a beauty pageant?"

(Modestly) "Oh, it was just for her school."

"She must love that crown."

"You know how kids are."

"She must be very talented."

"What a kind thing for you to say."

"I know you're proud of her."

"I am, but I try to stress that beauty isn't important."

It's imperative to say that last line with a straight face.

Above all else, keep reminding yourself that pride goeth before a fall. If you can't actually be humble, then at least have the good taste to pretend to be.

Never show the home videos of your child's latest accomplishment unless the audience insists, or at least says casually that they'd like to see the beauty pageant or ball game. If the audience seems bored, then turn off the DVD player (or VHS, depending on your child's age).

Or at least offer to turn it off. Only show the high points--namely your offspring--and wrap up the process as soon as possible. Try to tie it in with THEIR children if possible, but NEVER compare if your kids seem better at whatever it is. If you can't be humble, then at least be kind.

And if they bring out pictures, newspaper clippings, videos, or life-size graven images of their children, then, by all means, act thrilled and excited and compliment them on having such outstanding off-spring. The more you gush over theirs, the more they'll gush over yours.

If they have no children, then shut up about yours as soon as possible and ask them about their dog, cat, donkey, boat, car, house, job, sewing class, or whatever, and QUIT BRAGGING. I know it's tough when your kids really are so superior, but try. You may find that you gain friends who will actually ask you about your kids and, more importantly, care about the answer, thus giving you the chance to brag until your heart's content.

Grandparents, however, are generally the exception to all of the above rules. Grandparents are usually worse than parents when it comes to shameless bragging, so lay it on as thick as you like when talking to your parents or in-laws.

No need to hide behind false modesty. Make them copies of pictures and videos. Clip newspaper articles and send them a dozen or two copies. Relate all the particulars in excruciating detail. These are people who appreciate your child's accomplishments as much as, if not more than, you.

Then call back after they've had a chance to share the news with their friends and neighbors. After all, what good is it to have such accomplished children if you have no one to tell.

BIRTHING THE BABY

or

**I Don't Care What You Say,
This Is Strictly Woman's Work**

I can't speak for all men, or even for most men, but I personally LOVED being present for each of my three children's births, and I am absolutely convinced that my presence helped my wife through the labor and birth process. If you can be there for the conception, then you should be supportive enough to be there for the birth, whether or not you have a squeamish stomach.

Bringing a new life into the world is a beautiful experience, and men who miss it have missed more than they'll ever know. I understand that some men fear they'll faint or make fools of themselves, but it's important to know what their wives go through to give birth.

Our third child was born under the care of a nurse-midwife. The baby was born in a very small, rural hospital, and the mid-wife didn't arrive until the baby's head was half-way out.

Were we concerned? Not in the least. My wife and I had already discussed ME delivering the baby (or catching the baby, as we said, for we believed that our baby would deliver herself with a little help from my wife, and my main task would be to keep the child from falling on the floor.)

When labor began in the middle of the night, we didn't rush. We had to wait for someone to arrive to care for our other two children, and then we had about a thirty-minute drive to the hospital.

My wife was thirsty, so we stopped for apple juice on the way to the hospital. Not knowing when I'd have a chance to eat, we also stopped at the drive-thru of a fast food restaurant for a chicken biscuit for me. Even though we had pre-registered at the hospital, there was a mix-up at the hospital, and my wife was in hard labor by the time we finally arrived at the birthing room.

The mid-wife had been called, but had not yet arrived. The early-morning sun was peeking through the clouds, my wife felt "empowered," and I was setting up the video camera as my wife went to collect a urine sample requested by the nurse.

"The baby's coming!" my wife yelled.

The nurse wisely decided that a urine sample was unnecessary and began helping my wife to the birthing bed.

"Not yet!" I cried. "I don't have the camera set up!"

Determined not to let this be our only birth uncaught on videotape, I set up the tri-pod and camera as fast as I could, using a tasteful side view that showed nothing "personal" and hurried into position to "catch." My wife was gently pushing the baby's head out by this time and I was ready. Only the nurses seemed slightly panicky.

Suddenly, the door opened, the midwife walked in, saw what was happening, and explained, "That's great!"

She then checked to make sure the umbilical wasn't around the baby's neck. (It wasn't, but why didn't I think to do that?) Moments later the baby was out. I "caught" her and handed her to my wife. The midwife helped clean everyone up, and we left the hospital after my wife took a bath and ate lunch.

All in all, we were in the hospital about eight hours, including the time for me to go home, get the other two kids, and bring them to welcome their little sister to her new life. My wife took no medication whatsoever and needed no stitches.

The nurse-midwife experience was wonderful for us. My wife said that the nurse-midwife made her feel empowered enough that she felt that she and I could deliver that baby in the car if necessary, without the mid-wife even being present. We weren't nervous, and we were looking forward to the experience.

Keep in mind that this was our third child. The second had also been born without "benefit" of pain medication, although an OB-GYN delivered the baby in a much larger, urban hospital. The staff present at the second birth actually stood around with arms folded, offering no help or support to my wife for quite some time.

The doctor wanted to break the water, which we opposed, in order to speed things along. This was before the use of Pitocin became commonplace. As an aside, I strongly suggest you research this potentially dangerous drug before using.

Back to our story. Earlier, when my wife was already in hard labor, the nurses had actively opposed my wife walking around the room. We had insisted that the only monitoring be done externally and that possibly prompted their reluctance to let my wife do what felt right for her during this time. We felt that we had to fight to simply give birth as naturally as possible, and this played a large part in our decision to use a nurse-midwife for the next delivery.

The birth of our first child was very "conventional." We called the doctor, and he instructed us to first come to his office. He examined my wife and sent us to the hospital, whereupon she was promptly medicated. Although I have no proof, I'm convinced that this medication caused our baby to sleep for the first twenty-four hours after her birth and to cry for the next twenty-four hours.

After arriving in the birthing room, I was asked to leave while they put the epidural into my wife's spine. I've often wondered why they didn't want me to see what she also could not see.

As my wife's contractions were being monitored, it was obvious that the pain medications caused the contractions to slow dramatically. My wife was now unable to feel her body realistically and had to be told when to push. She was unable to gauge her own body's contractions and ruptured a blood vessel in her eye.

An episiotomy was done, and countless stitches were required. My wife said later that it took longer to heal from the episiotomy than from the actual birth.

While I realize that it's vitally important to monitor the baby's heart rate, etc., I personally had much disdain for the "corkscrew" monitor that the physician literally screwed into the scalp of our first child.

The ridiculous thing worked itself loose, and the doctor simply reached into the birth canal and screwed it in again, now leaving two wounds in our child's head. When I questioned this, I was assured that babies don't feel pain like adults. Whether or not this is so, we insisted the monitoring be done differently when our other children were born.

At one point the monitor attached to the corkscrew failed to work, causing great alarm on the part of my wife. She feared that the baby was dead until they simply wheeled in another monitor which accurately recorded the baby's heart rate.

Similar thoughts raced through my mind, but as I was not under the influence of narcotics, I assumed that if indeed the baby's heart had stopped beating, a caesarian section would be immediately performed, and I took comfort in the fact that no such preparations were underway. While I tend to believe that many such procedures are unnecessary, I do value medical technology when necessary.

It was the fear of possible complications that prompted our desire to have our third child born in a hospital, as opposed to having a home birth, which has a certain romantic appeal and avoids a lot of uncomfortable travel. We wanted medical technology to be close at hand in the remote possibility that an unforeseen problem might arise.

One of the most interesting differences between a traditional physician-directed birth and a nurse-midwife-directed birth was in attitude. My wife absolutely loved her physician, who was also her gynecologist, and had never met the nurse-midwife prior to her pregnancy. Yet, the nurse-midwife made her feel powerful, in control, and more than capable of birthing a baby, even if she had to do it all by herself.

On the other hand, traditional medicine seems to view women as helpless creatures who are unable to birth children without relinquishing control to the medical establishment, which generally means letting a big, strong man take charge of the entire process. The nurses merely do the doctor's bidding and don't dare suggest alternatives.

When our second child was soon to be born, the doctor finally gave permission for my wife to more-or-less do it her way. At this point, one older nurse, who had worked in rural areas, took over, offering the first active guidance and support to my wife. The nurse enthusiastically offered suggestions for breathing, pushing, etc., and gave much-needed emotional support.

The physician even got into the spirit of the event and began offering specific, concrete advice on pushing, etc. This was after a prolonged period of everyone standing around with their arms folded, waiting for my wife to come to her senses and let the doctor do what he'd been trained to do. Prior to the doctor's realization that my wife can be very stubborn and giving his "permission" for her to give birth the way SHE wanted, the older nurse was eerily silent.

However, before you and your wife decide on the type of birthing experience that the three of you (counting the baby) would like to have, consult with your physician, your mid-wife if you're considering one, and read up on the subject.

Get an education before you make a decision. Talk to others about their experiences, and try to understand possible risks. My wife was blessed to have three normal, relatively easy pregnancies and deliveries. All women are not so fortunate, and I know several mothers and children who would not be alive today without modern technology and highly skilled doctors. Don't make hasty decisions, and be as informed as possible.

Every woman's pregnancy is unique, and some risk is inherent in every birth. If you must err, it's always better to err on the side of caution.

If you do choose to videotape the birth, which I personally highly recommend, remember that you may want to show it to others. I suggest placing the camera to your wife's side or near her shoulder, so you're looking down at what's going on. You may not see the head actually emerging, but you can capture the baby immediately after it's born, and you won't have everyone discussing whether or not your wife was shaved for the birth.

Some people don't want to be distracted by fumbling with a camera, yet are reluctant to have another person present for such a private moment. One solution is to set up the shot, with the camera set to capture a wide angle, start it running, and forget about it. The main danger here is being unaware if a problem occurs or forgetting about the camera and standing in front of it as I did during part of our first child's birth.

Immediately after the baby is born, you can zoom in for close-ups. It's also a nice touch to "interview" nurses, doctors, or anyone else present. This can be done before or after the delivery, or both.

And don't forget your wife. While she may not feel like answering questions during labor pains, you may find her more cooperative if you time your questions between contractions. You may want to step in front of the camera and say a few words yourself. After all, the father has a significant part in this entire process.

Above all else, remember that YOU ARE THERE TO SUPPORT YOUR WIFE. Any and all camera work should be secondary. Your main job is to hold her hand, wipe her brow, help her count and/or breathe, and to provide loving emotional support. She should be the focus of the activities, and you must be careful not to be distracted by cameras.

If pictures are important to you, be sure to also have a still camera or use your cell phone. Have a nurse take a family shot with you included, and, naturally, take lots of pictures of mother and baby. You'll want these for photo albums, baby books, and grandparents, and it's also insurance in case the video doesn't work for some reason. If you want added insurance, bring along two still cameras and take pictures with both.

After all, everyone knows you can never have too many pictures of a baby, particularly if it's your first. And remember, if you don't do equally for all other children, you will forever be accused of loving one more than the rest. I constantly told this to my wife as she took endless rolls of film of our first baby and has diligently tried, with questionable success, to prove to the other two that she also took countless pictures of them drooling, sleeping, laughing, crying, eating, and, yes, even lying naked on a sheepskin rug--bottoms up, of course.

"Why do you have more pictures of her than me?"

"I don't think we have more pictures of your sister."

"Yes, you do. You must have a hundred albums full of
  pictures of her and only one half-full of me!"

"We don't have a hundred picture albums all together."

"Almost!"

"If we do have more pictures of your sister, it's only
 because she was born first."

"Did you camera break after I was born?"

"Of course not. It's just that first babies are very
  special."

"You love her more than me!"

"No, we don't. We love all of you the same."

"No, you don't!"

"Yes, we do."

"Then why didn't you take any pictures of me?"

"We have lots of pictures of you. Look at this. Here's
  one of you eating ice cream."

"But she's in the picture, too!"

"Here's one of you alone."

"That's her foot!"

"That's not a foot, it's a...a...a..."

"It's her foot!"

"Well, what if it is? It's your face."

"My eyes are closed."

"Well, that's not our fault. Here's another picture of you
  with your eyes open."

"That's her standing behind me!"

"Well, Dear, we can't help it if you were standing in
 front of your sister when we took your picture."

"How come I'm not in any of those pictures of her?"

"You weren't born yet."

"You don't love me!"

"Yes, we love you very much."

"Then why wasn't I born first?"

You'll never win, so the best thing to do is pull out the camera or the cell
phone and take an endless number of pictures of the second child--unless, of
course, the first child is present.

If he or she is, then wait and take the pictures later. Get two copies and an
extra picture album to give to the second child for his or her very own. It
won't make up for the missing baby pictures, but it will help even things out a
bit.

Just be prepared for child number one to pitch a fit when she sees what her
little brother has.

DOING LAUNDRY

or

Laundry, Laundry Everywhere,
But Not a Sock to Wear

Where does it all come from? Does it really multiply in the laundry hamper, or do nasty little gnomes add dirty towels and mismatched socks late at night while everyone is sleeping? How can such little people (i.e. children) create such big piles of permanently stained, eternally wrinkled, ill-fitting clothing without really trying?

As we ponder these and other senseless, answerless questions about sock-eating washing machines, we should pay homage to the woman of yore who beat wet clothes against rocks while holding a baby at her breast. (Thoughts such as these help when putting stain remover on little Johnny's shirt for the fourth time in a futile attempt to remove those blackberry stains.)

Let's be honest about it. Doing laundry is a chore with a capital "C." I don't mind putting the clothes in the washer, particularly since I only rarely separate the whites from the colors, and I don't find it too troublesome to transfer the clean (I use that word loosely) clothes to the dryer, but I LOATHE ironing, sorting, folding, and putting away. While I don't see why the kids can't get their clothes directly from the laundry basket next to the dryer, my wife feels their clothing needs a greater sense of order. I don't mind folding bath towels and putting them away, and obvious things like dresses and shirts are only minor annoyances. It's sock-sorting that absolutely drives me up the wall. We have three children, all of whom are roughly two years apart in age, and the socks are only slightly different in size. I could probably eventually figure it all out if their feet didn't keep growing. Then the socks (at least sometimes) become the property of the next child down the line, and I become completely confused and disoriented.

I have read nifty suggestions, such as using a safety pin to pin the socks together. My wife bought some silly-looking plastic double-ringed things that supposedly keep the socks together. I have even heard it suggested to roll the dirty socks into each other before washing, as if rolled-up socks from our children would EVER get clean.

To be completely honest, I must confess that I hate sorting my own socks. All the white ones look alike and all the dark ones look alike. What's so bad about wearing one black sock and one navy blue sock anyway? Does anyone really look that closely at my ankles?

I had a friend who once spray-painted a pair of white socks black while wearing them because he had no clean black socks to wear to a formal dinner party. Never mind that the paint leaked through his socks, turning his ankles black. Maybe someone should market socks that come with six colors of spray paint. You'd only need to own one pair and simply spray them whatever color you needed.

Speaking of socks, have you ever wondered where all the lost socks in the world end up? I don't care what the Maytag repairman says, you'll never convince me that washing machines don't have a hearty appetite for socks. Our washer is definitely a "sampler," because it never eats more than one of the pair. Perhaps it also eats an occasional pair of underpants or panties, but it takes longer to miss these items than the obvious lonely unmatched sock.

Where do all these odd socks go? Are the sewers of New York City filled with millions and millions of unmatched socks, or do they eventually make their way to the sea and the nesting sites of giant octopuses?

I don't recommend doing what I have been known to do with all the unsorted socks that survived the washing machine and dryer--namely, nothing. DON'T leave them in an empty laundry basket to be frantically searched through as your child stands nearby, wearing coat, hat, and gloves, but no socks. DON'T stuff them all in a drawer to be sorted at a later time that will never arrive. And above all else, DON'T leave them in the dryer to spend eternity drying again and again in hopes that they will someday miraculously mate with the proper match.

Face it--you've got to sit down and sort those suckers. You might try doing it during the evening news or while dinner is cooking. If you're really desperate you could try leaving them in a basket in the bathroom and sort them while watching a youngster in the tub or even while sitting on the john, although I don't recommend either.

If your kids are old enough (thirty, maybe) you could try to get each to sort his or her own socks. I don't think you should wait until your wife does it, although this has happened occasionally in our home. Remember, people who work all day outside the home don't want to work all night (or all weekend) inside the home.

If you don't believe me, just ask my wife.

Getting away from socks and back to laundry in general, remember that the longer clothes stay in a cold dryer, the more wrinkled they become. Ideally, as soon as they are dry, take all clothes that might need ironing and hang them up IMMEDIATELY. Many wrinkles will fall out.

Putting them back in the dryer for a couple of minutes can often help get out wrinkles, as can hanging the garment in a steamy bathroom while you shower. I've heard that using a hand-held hair drying can get out some wrinkles, but I've never tried it personally. Even if some wrinkles are left, they'll be easier to iron out or less noticeable if you decide to wear a jacket and not worry about a couple to wrinkles in the back of the shirt.

And whatever you do, avoid 100% cotton if you want to avoid ironing. Blends and permanent press are the ticket to an iron-free life.

I've heard that some people iron sheets, pillow cases, and underwear, but I'm sure these are the same people who use a hair comb to comb their lawns. If nature had intended us to wear ironed underwear, then we wouldn't have such wrinkled bodies. I personally hate to iron and avoid it as much as humanly possible.

One last thing about laundry. When I first began staying home full-time and assumed the bulk of the laundry duties, my wife found fault with my laundry techniques, such as the lack of separation between whites and colors, my lack of judgment as to water temperatures, bleaches, detergents, and softeners. We found a solution that has worked well for us. My wife does her own laundry or sends it to the cleaners, and I try to take care of mine and the kids'. She isn't overwhelmed with sheer volume, particularly since I still wash some of her everyday things, yet she can be certain that her nicer things are cared for in a manner she finds suitable.

She keeps her dirty clothes in a separate basket in her closet while the rest of the family's dirty clothes go into the laundry hamper in the main bathroom. I wash anything in that hamper, even her things, but never anything in the basket in her closet. My wife still does the family wash sometimes, as I can barely keep up. This flexibility keeps either of us from feeling completely overwhelmed by the constant barrage of dirty laundry generated by an active family of five.

"I don't want to wear those pants. I want to wear the
 ones I got for my birthday."

"They're dirty."

"Wash them, then."

"We don't have time. Wear these instead."

"Those are for kids."

"You are a kid."

"I'm almost a teenager!"

"You're only five."

"Five is almost ten and ten is a teenager."

"Thirteen is a teenager."

"Well, I'm not wearing those ugly pants. I won't wear
  anything."

"You're too old to be naked."

"You never let me do anything!"

"Here, wear these jeans."

"Will you give me candy?"

"No."

"Will you buy me a toy?"

"No."

"No deal."

"I didn't know we were making deals. What about these jogging pants?"

"They're too hot."

"What about these gray ones?"

"I want to wear the new ones!"

"All right, if they're not too dirty, you can wear them again."

"I'd rather have candy."

"Here they are. They look O.K. No one will notice that little spot. Or that one. Keep your shirt tail out."

"Never mind."

"What?"

"I'll wear these."

"That's the first pair I showed you."

"I'll wear them even if I am almost a teenager."

"Wouldn't you rather wear the new ones?"

"Not unless I can have candy."

"Now, where are your socks?"

You may want to try to get your kids involved with doing the laundry. My first grader sometimes helps fold clothes, although she avoids trying to sort socks. My four-year-old likes to put the laundry soap in the washer, and the toddler likes to throw all the clothes, clean or dirty, on the floor.

Just keep reminding yourself: If you let them help when they first want to help, they'll still want to help when they're old enough to be of help.

At least I hope so.

A MAN ALONE

or

Oh, My, There's a Man in Here!

If you're a stay-at-home dad and you happen to have one or more daughters, you will inevitably find yourself in a room filled with nothing but girls and their mothers.

I found myself in just this situation when my six-year-old daughter entered a beauty contest at her elementary school. Even though the pageant was in the evening, my wife was unable to attend due to a work conflict. She managed to come home long enough to roll my daughter's hair and help get her dressed, but could not go to the school with our daughter. We had a sitter for the other children and off I went to be a stage mother.

We were running a little late, so when we arrived all the other girls were ready, except for the last-minute make-up and hair adjustments. I frantically began taking out the rollers when a kind-hearted high school girl offered to help fix my daughter's hair.

As we unrolled hair, which her mother had rolled earlier, I looked up and saw several mothers staring at us. I wasn't sure if they approved or disapproved, but they certainly looked confused. Only a couple of mothers, whom I knew fairly well, even spoke to me. Most were either totally focused on their own daughters or were trying to not notice that I wasn't a woman.

I didn't detect any outright hostility, but I wasn't embraced as one of the group, either. Perhaps they were perplexed. Perhaps they wondered if their own husbands would ever allow themselves to be in this position. Perhaps they thought I was a very butch woman. But whatever they thought, they said nothing unkind, and, for the most part, mostly ignored me.

No one asked why I was there or where my wife was, although I volunteered the information to a few people. With the exception of the high school student, who knew my daughter fairly well, no one offered to help. Maybe this was because I appeared to have everything under control, or maybe because their daughters were in competition with mine and they were grateful a possibly inept man was doing hair and lipstick. Basically, I was ignored, like a picked-over tomato at the grocery store.

"Mildred, did you see? There's a man in there!"

"A man? What's he doing?"

"Hair and make-up!"

"Is he a hair-dresser?"

"I don't think so."

"Who is he?"

"I think he's a father."

"A father? You've got to be kidding!"

"I'm serious. I think he's helping his daughter get
  ready."

"I can't believe it! I've never heard of such a thing! And
  in this town!"

"My husband certainly would never do that."

"Mine either!"

"Lousy scum!"

"That man?"

"No, my husband. I think that man is perfectly
  wonderful. I just hope his daughter loses the pageant."

"Oh, she will. Can you imagine? A father? What could
  be more ridiculous!"

Regardless of what everyone thought, I was doing what I needed to do, just as my wife was doing what she needed to do, for the benefit of our family. If the mothers thought I was odd, so be it.

Besides, my daughter won.

Shopping for Girls

or

No, I'm Not a Woman With a Deep Voice

On the day of the before-mentioned beauty pageant, I had to shop for a crinoline slip for my six-year-old daughter. As I was rushed for time, I called a local department store to see if they had such a thing in stock in a size six. The young woman in the girls' department obviously wasn't used to dealing with men when discussing children's slips.

"Do you have puffy slips for a six-year- old?" I asked.

"Yes, Ma'am, we have one," she replied.

Being more rushed than offended, I only lowered my voice slightly.

"The kind that go under a beauty pageant dress," I said.

The young woman hesitated momentarily before answering.

"We just have one, a size eight..." she said, not finishing.

I knew she was unsure whether to say ma'am or sir, so she chose the wise way and said nothing.

When I picked up the slip later that day, she did not seem the least bit surprised that I was male. I told her that I'd called about the size eight slip, and she merely smiled, reached under the counter, and handed me a crinoline slip.

She did, however, give me a five-dollar discount, saying that the slip had been returned.

I wonder if that's the real reason.

RAISING YOUR OWN CHILDREN

or

If You Don't Want to Raise Them,
Then Why Have Them?

This is the chapter I edited severely when I dusted off the old manuscript. Times had changed, and almost all couples now work out of perceived necessity. It is not for me to judge whether or not this is truly necessary, and I have softened my outlook on working parents.

However, this book is aimed at men who choose to be stay-at-home dads and raise their children. A parent staying home with the children is today's rarity, while, when I was a child, it was the norm.

Of course, back in those ancient times, it was invariably the mother who stayed at home and raised the children. A man doing so in those days would have been thought of as an anomaly at the very least. I shudder to think what else.

So I have decided to not rail against parents who work and just focus on the intended audience. In no way do I want to add guilt to lives that are already stressed to the max. For both parents to work full-time while raising children is a formidable challenge and deserves a book of its own.

I have kept portions of my original chapter, but have done some heavy editing. Family life changes over time, and whether or not these changes are for the better can only be judged in retrospect. I applaud families who can manage one parent to stay at home with the children, be it mother or father. But I will not disparage families who choose to do otherwise for whatever reasons. We all do what we feel is right at the time.

"Let's have a baby."

"Do you think we should?

"Yes. We're getting older. We shouldn't put it off any

longer."

"Can we afford to have a baby?"

"I know daycare is expensive. And we'd need to turn
 that extra bedroom into a nursery."

"We'd have to buy a crib. A pretty one, with a canopy."

"Diapers aren't cheap. Especially the name brands. Do
 they make designer diapers?"

"Our baby can only have the best."

"We'd have to buy all new clothes. I couldn't let our
 baby wear anything used."

"Formula costs a bundle…unless we breast-feed."

"Too much trouble. We'd want to redecorate the room."

"We'd have to paint the whole house. I'm sure we'd
 have lots of company coming over."

"We'd need a bigger car."

"Maybe this yard is too small. Should we buy a new
 house?"

"Every child needs a pony."

"And music lessons."

"Only the best college for our child."

"We'll have to rent a clown for the baby's first birthday."

"I'll have to buy some new clothes."

"Maybe a house by the seashore."

"We'll have to put in a swimming pool."

"And a tennis court."

"Our child should have the best opportunities."

"Private schools."

"Summer camp."

"A car at age sixteen."

"Trips abroad."

"We'll have to join a country club."

"Riding lessons."

"And one of those things."

"What things?"

"Those things for the nursery with the padded tops."

"A diaper changer?"

"Absolutely! How can you change a baby's diaper
  without a diaper changer?"

"How does a diaper changer change diapers anyway?"

"No idea."

"Can we afford daycare?"

"Do we have a choice? Somebody has to take care of
  the kid, and it costs a lot to have the best."

"And our baby is worth it!"

"Absolutely!"

"Maybe I can take a second job on weekends."

"I could work in sales in the evenings, too."

"Do they have night-time daycare?"

"Probably. Can we afford it?"

"If we both work two jobs, then we ought to be able to
  pay for childcare."

"After all, nothing is too good for our baby."

"Nothing."

What does it matter if the poor child rarely sees her parents? After all, she does have a pony.

And a diaper changer.

I know many would insist that childcare is a woman's domain, implying that women have more inborn ability for caring for offspring than the men who sired them. While not wanting to argue with tradition, I believe that men are, at least in theory, completely capable of caring for children. I believe that fathers are capable of giving love and of being nurturing, sometimes as much as the best mothers.

It wasn't that many years ago that MOST women stayed home with the kids while the family survived on only one income. Perhaps they drove a modest car and lived in a so-so neighborhood, but the couple raised their children themselves, without daycare or live-in nannies. If sheer financial survival is dependent on two incomes today, then adequate daycare is not what we should be writing our congresspersons about.

Being a parent is difficult. Being a good parent is near-to-impossible. But it's easy to love a child, and all you can do is the best you can do. If that's not good enough, then at least you'll have the satisfaction of knowing that you tried and that you did the best you knew how to do at the time. Your kids will probably think it wasn't good enough, and maybe it wasn't.

But at least you tried.

"I know you're disappointed in how he turned out."

"I wouldn't say disappointed. Surprised might be a
      better word."

"No, I think disappointed is the word I'd use if he
        were my son."
"Well, he's not your son."

"My son is a doctor."

"You're very blessed."

"I'm not ashamed of my son."

"Neither am I."

"You're not?"

"My son has never been in trouble. He's never even
        had a parking ticket."

"As I said before, you are very blessed."

"How can you deal with the shame and guilt?"

"Why would I feel shame and guilt?"

"Well, I certainly would."

"You son made sound decisions. I'm sure you are
        very proud."

"You have my sympathy."

"Well, if I ever need it, thank you."

"You need it. You just don't know it."

"I have to go now. I'm visiting my son."

"Will you be able to hold back the tears?"

 "I'll bring a tissue just in case."

"You must love him very much."

"Of course I do, even if he is imperfect. After all,
        he is my child."

"That's so sweet. I think I may cry."

"You want to borrow my tissue?"

The following two chapters were added recently, after my children were grown. They deal with a sensitive subject, and I do not claim to be an expert on child-rearing, only a parent. As parents, we make choices, we make decisions, we generally try to do what we think is best for our children, our families, and, occasionally, for ourselves.

TO FIB OR NOT TO FIB

or

How Much Information is Too Much?

Lying to children--is it good? Bad? Necessary? In times past I think it was more common to tell falsehoods to children, be it that babies were found in cabbage patches or brought by storks, or hiding the fact that the child was adopted at birth. Now, most so-called authorities say parents should be honest with children, but to answer questions or give explanations at a level understandable to the child based on the child's age. This seems reasonable to me.

I once read an amusing story about a child asking her mother, "Where did I come from?" The mother, thinking this was the time to discuss sex with her daughter, went into a long explanation of biology and reproduction, being as accurate as possible within the context of the child's age. The daughter listened, and when the mother, proud of her explanation, finally paused, the girl said, "No, where did I come from? Susie said she came from Boston."

I agree that children should generally be given accurate answers to questions, although the parent has to decide where to draw the line when the questions become personal. What do you say if you child asks if you ever used drugs or drove after drinking or ever stole anything or had sex before marriage?

If your youthful life was less than perfect you could choose to use this as a teaching moment on avoiding pitfalls during the folly of youth. Or you may feel this simply is not your child's business and refuse to answer, which may lead the child the think the worse. Or you can choose to tell a lie.

I have no answer to this dilemma. I think a lot of factors should be considered, the age and maturity level of the child, how well the parent has dealt with the youthful indiscretions, and if the parent simply wants the child to have this information. Will the child tell all her friends what Daddy used to do in college?

Of course there are virtuous parents with nothing in their backgrounds they would not want published on the front page of the local newspaper, but most people have at least one incident in their lives they are not proud of. Does you child need to know this to better understand you and life? Or would it be better to wait until the child is older to share this information?

"Daddy, did you ever kiss a girl?"

"Yes, Dear, I kiss your mommy all the time."

"Did you ever kiss another girl?"

"Er, uh, yes."

"Does Mommy know you kissed another girl?"

"Er, uh, yes. But it was a long time ago, before I
     knew your mommy."

"Mommy said she kissed another boy."

"Really? When?"
"Yesterday."

"What!? Your mommy kissed someone yesterday?"

"I don't know. She told me yesterday."

"Oh. That's different."

"I'm never going to kiss a boy."

"Good."

"Or a girl."

"Even better."

"Or a frog."

"I don't blame you."

"Susie said you get babies when you kiss a boy."

"It's been known to happen."

"Did you and that girl get a baby?"

"What girl?"

"The one you kissed before you knew Mommy."

"No, definitely not. Is it time for you to go
        outside?"

"It's raining outside. How many times did you kiss
        that other girl?"

"Go outside anyway. You can skip your bath."

"How many times do you have to kiss a boy to have
        a baby?"

"Er, uh, I don't know. Want to watch cartoons?"

"What if you kiss him on the cheek? Does that
        count?"

"I don't know. Don't you want to look at a book?"

"I'm going to ask Susie. She knows all about
        babies! You don't know anything."

You might as well sit down and have a short talk about reproduction, keeping
it at the child's level. A good time to teach anything is when the child is
ready to learn.

Ever notice how children raised on farms have a better understanding of
biology and reproduction? They also tend to be better able to deal with
death.

Birth and death are all part of life. People forget that grieving is also a
learned experience. I think living in the country was beneficial in many ways
for my children, but similar lessons can be learned from having a goldfish.

Don't be afraid to let your children learn to grieve. It'll help them later in life.

WHICH BRINGS US TO...

or

This Was The One I Hesitated To Write

In our culture, we tell children a lot of fables about fictional characters that we present as reality. Is this healthy? Have you ever wondered why do we do this?

It seems the more we strive to be honest with children about reproduction, predators, dangerous situations, and life in general, we cling ever more fervently to other fables we explain to children as truths.

Of course, this varies from home to home, but we generally no longer say storks leave babies in cabbage patches, while clinging to stories about fairies and elves and that most sacred of all cows, Santa Claus.

I would never tell parents how to raise their children. I can only speak for my wife and me, and I can't say with absolute certainty that our choices in this area were the best choices. But I do encourage all parents to sit down and think about these matters, to really think about this without prejudice, without undue emotions, looking rationally and logically. Don't be unduly influenced by culture or tradition or your mother's opinion.

My wife and I discussed this before having children, and it was one of the few things on which we actually agreed. We decided not to tell our children there were elves, unicorns, leprechauns, Easter Bunnies, fairies, tooth or otherwise, Jack Frost, and even Santa Claus.

We simply said these were all make-believe characters, like Batman and Superman. One of my children later said that when he was a young child he wasn't 100% certain that Batman was not real.

I guess we didn't explain it well enough.

Our children still got ample Christmas presents under the tree and still found money under their pillows where a missing tooth had been, but they simply knew who put them there. They got as many Christmas presents as their friends, and they seemed just as excited, but they knew who bought them. We simply told them the truth, without fanfare, without malice, without self-righteousness.

I know many readers will disagree with this, and I respect that. Our children were instructed to never tell any of their peers there was no tooth fairy or Santa Claus. As adults, they have all told me that they never did, although my daughter said she felt sorry for children who believed in these things. I guess it's like knowing that storks don't really bring babies when all your friends think they do.
My daughter says what she missed most about knowing Santa's identity was not being able to bake cookies and leave them for Santa to eat. I pointed out that daddies like cookies, too.

One issue about the Santa Claus myth that troubles me is the disparity in giving. I have wondered what poor children think when they see the modest gifts "Santa" brought them and compare that to the elaborate gifts given to children from wealthier families. Do these poor children think Santa Claus likes rich kids more than poor kids? Or that rich kids behave better? It seems that Santa favors the rich. I wonder if anyone has ever done research on these types of topics and how these obvious disparities affect the children.

"What did Santa Claus bring you?"

"I got some clothes, a book, and some candy."

"What else?"

"My grandmother gave me ten dollars."

"What else did Santa bring you?"

"Nothing."

"You must have been very bad last year."

"I don't think so. I didn't get a bundle of switches
        or a lump of coal."

"Santa brought me a bicycle, a scooter, lots and lots
        of designer clothes, those sneakers I saw on TV, a

new phone, three board games, a soccer ball, two
video games, and other stuff. He gave me
everything on my list! I can't even remember all
of it."

"Wow. I've never gotten all that stuff."

"Santa brings me things like that every year."

"Really? Santa must really like you. Better than
me, I guess."

"Yeah, I think you're right."
"I feel like crying. You have a bigger house than
me, a better car, a swimming pool, lots more
money and clothes, you go on fancy vacations, and
now even Santa Claus likes you better, too!"

"Yeah."

"What's wrong with me?"

"There's nothing wrong with you. You're just poor,
that's all. There's nothing wrong with being poor.
It just means you're not rich."

"Everybody likes rich people better. Even Santa
Claus."

"I like you, even if you're poor."

"Santa Claus doesn't."
"You want to come over and play one of the   video
games Santa brought me? I'll let you win."

All families must decide for themselves whether or not to perpetuate these
near-universal myths of childhood. I can see both sides of this, and I don't
expect anyone to change his or her views based on my opinions. All I ask is
for parents to think about this, and, if religious, to pray about it. Then do as
your conscience dictates.

COOKING

or

If The Cook Won't Eat It,
Then Neither Will I

Cooking. Some people love to do it; some people loathe it. I personally find it to be a creative outlet, a chance to express myself and to prepare exactly what I want, even if no one else is thrilled with soy burgers or mustard sandwiches.

As I've said before, your spouse will appreciate a home-cooked meal at least occasionally, and so will you. The kids may prefer a Happy Meal, but that's another chapter.

But what do you do if you think you don't know how to cook? First of all, don't be intimidated. After all, the basic premise of cooking is to apply heat to raw food prior to eating, at least according to my brother. Of course, there are subtle nuances, but if it gets hot enough for long enough you can probably call it done. It may not be edible, but it will be done.

The next step, particularly if you feel insecure in the kitchen, is to buy a good cookbook. There are countless good cookbooks on the market, but one old stand-by is *THE JOY OF COOKING* by Ima Rombauer and Marion Rombauer Becker, which has been around for decades with various revisions.

You may want cookbooks that specialize in ethnic, vegetarian, healthy, or desserts, but *THE JOY OF COOKING* is a good basic guide to get you started. And, of course, any recipe imaginable in on the internet.

Don't forget that recipes can be used as a general guide, and you can make changes as desired or as necessary based on ingredients on hand. Cooking is a creative art form, and recipes are not carved in stone. Dare to experiment. Some will be successful, some will be best forgotten. Repeat the successes, let the failures be humorous stories your children will tell their children. But, if feeling insecure, just follow the recipe to the letter. As my cousin used to say, anyone can cook if he or she can read.

While fats are no longer totally taboo and some are now considered health-promoting, trans-fats are still best avoided. Read labels. Educate yourself. Trans-fats tend to show up in margarine and in desserts, but can be found virtually anywhere. Substitute applesauce, pureed figs or mashed pumpkin for margarine in a dessert and cut sugar accordingly since all these things contains sugar, even if from fruit.

If you want to cut back on fat in general to save calories, you may want to add additional herbs and spices. Smother it in tomato sauce and/or fat-free or reduced fat cheese. Steam it, bake it, or grill it. Or just serve it dry and give everyone unlimited water. I'd personally rather eat dry food than have by-pass surgery.

"What is this?"

"Vegetarian spaghetti."

"Why are the noodles so brown?"

"They're whole wheat."

"You eat this?"

"No, I just toss it into the air and see if it sticks to the
 ceiling."

"Is that supposed to be garlic bread?"

"It is garlic bread."

"It looks like whole wheat."

"Imagine that."

"Why is it so dry?"

"No butter."

"Not even margarine?"

"Especially no margarine. Lots of garlic."

"I don't think I can swallow something so dry."

"Chew it first."

"I don't have enough saliva."

"Drink some water."

"I had better food the last time I was in the hospital."

"Try it."

"Very well. I'll taste it."

"Well? What do you think?"

"It has a lot of flavor, if you like garlic."

"Do you like it?"

"I don't dislike it especially."

"Does that mean you like it?"

"It means I didn't gag."

"Would you like a little more?"

"Only a little."

"You do like it."

"I'm still getting used to it."

"You'll like it when you get used to it."

"Doubtful."

"You don't have to finish it if you don't like it."

"I've had worse."

"It's very good for you."

"Can I have some more garlic bread?"

"It's not too dry?"

"Yes, it is, but I'll eat it anyway."

"I think you like my vegetarian spaghetti."

"I'm just trying to be polite."

"Would you like the recipe?"

"I'd have to add butter. Or at least margarine."

"Then it wouldn't be healthy."

"I could use less."

"Why use any?"

"Because everyone cooks that way."

"I don't."

"If it's so bad, why do they serve it in hospitals?"

"You tell me."

"Because they want patients to eat and get well."

"Wouldn't patients get well eating healthy food?"

"Absolutely not. Healthy food would only make them
  sicker."

"Why would that be?"

"Because they're not used to it. Give them all this
  healthy stuff and their poor, abused bodies would
  revolt."

"You've done research?"

"It's only a theory. Could I have some more of those
  brown noodles?"

"There are no more."

"I was starting to like them."

"I'll give you the recipe if you promise not to add
  butter."

"Not even margarine?"

"Especially not margarine."

"Do I have to tell anyone?"

"No."

"Good. I don't want to offend anyone."

"Who would you offend?"

"Margarine eaters."

"I see."

"Some people eat margarine for their health. It used to
  be healthier than butter."

"Margarine is not healthy."

"Well, don't tell margarine eaters."

"Why not?"

"Ignorance is bliss."

"Oh."

"Besides, it tastes good."

"Ignorance tastes good?"

"Compared to dry bread."

"I'll remember that."

"What's for dessert?"

"Chocolate chip oat bran muffins."

"Is that healthy?"

"It's healthier than packaged pastries."

"Greasy garlic bread and white noodles are healthier
than packaged pastries."

"Which would you rather have?"

"Can I chew on a stick of margarine while I think about
it?"

"I only have butter."

A few years ago, I began reading books and magazines about health and diet. I slowly began to realize that if I continued eating as I was eating I would be enjoying it more for a lot less years. I gradually began incorporating healthier versions of my favorite foods. Eventually, I started substituting vegetarian products occasionally and tried to cut back on my biggest weakness--fried everything.

Then the oddest thing happened. I found that I actually starting liking the vegetarian versions of favorite foods. I still liked the unhealthy version, but I also liked the new foods. Sometimes I'd have one, sometimes the other.

As time went by, I noticed that I was eating healthier foods more and more, while eliminating many of the unhealthy meals. Now I find that I actually crave certain vegetarian dishes. While I can still appreciate a well-fried chicken leg, I can also enjoy a black bean burger.

I doubt that I'll ever eliminate meat completely, but most research indicates that vegetarians are generally healthier than their meat eating counterparts.

Vegetarian isn't necessarily low-calorie, particularly desserts that are full of sugar, and vegetarians can still get fat if they pig out all the time.

If you decide to improve your diet, make changes gradually unless you have a pressing health reason. If you give up all your favorite foods at once, you'll probably go into withdrawal and decide that you'd rather be dead than live in constant denial.

Try a meat substitute for lunch one day a week, and, at the same time, make a conscious effort to create a healthier version of the unhealthy foods that you're still eating. After a couple of months, try the veggie meals twice a week. Gradually add more and more days until you've changed your lifestyle without even noticing.

You will probably need to eat mostly at home and do your own cooking. Unless you go to "health-food" type restaurants, most restaurant food will not win the healthy option award, be it your local fast food enterprise or the most expensive place in town.

Words to remember: YOU CAN COOK IT WITHOUT MARGARINE AND YOU CAN EAT IT WITHOUT RANCH DRESSING AND YOU MAY LIVE TO TELL ABOUT IT.

Try it for six months, and you may never want to go back.

RECIPES

or

Anybody Can Cook
If He Owns a Can Opener

ONCE IN A LIFETIME CHICKEN

When in doubt, cook chicken, unless you're a vegetarian. It tastes good no matter how you fix it. Just be sure to cook it all the way through. If there's blood on the bone or if the juices don't run clean, then keep cooking it. Beware of food-borne diseases, and be sure to wash everything with hot, soapy water.

I call one of my wife's favorite chicken dishes ONCE IN A LIFTIME CHICKEN because there is no real recipe. I start with chicken--any pieces you like--and I add a little of nearly everything and bake it for about an hour to an hour and a half at an oven temperature of about 350. Make certain it's done before you serve it so you won't make everyone sick.

I'm referring to making a sauce for the chicken when I say to add a little of "nearly everything." Start with whatever you have in the refrigerator. If you have some fruit juice, be it apple, orange, pineapple, or whatever, pour some in a bowl. No fruit juice? Vinegar, particularly apple cider vinegar, is a good beginning. You may want to add vinegar to your fruit juice if you have both available.

Do you have countless packets of sauces from fast food restaurants? We seem to collect these by the bagful. Add taco sauce (hot or mild or both), ketchup, mustard, barbeque, sweet & sour, soy, honey, horseradish, or nearly anything you like the taste of.

Look in the refrigerator. Got half a can of leftover chili, hot dog or otherwise? Toss it in. Leftover spaghetti sauce or pizza sauce? Now's a perfect time to get rid of it. You can use carrots, small pieces of potatoes, onions, mushrooms, even baked beans. This is no time to be reticent.

Peppers, in any form, add flavor, as do countless seasonings. Like Italian?
How about curry or cumin or fennel? Don't forget garlic and ginger root.
This is your chance to be creative. Just cut it up and toss it in.

How much to use? How highly seasoned do you like your food? I love spicy
food and I never measure amounts. I just dump a little in. And then a little
more. Use common sense, but don't be too cautious. If it's not what you
hoped for this time, just change it a little next time. Sooner or later you'll hit a
recipe that everyone will love.

The only trouble is, you'll never be able to duplicate it exactly, as this is
ONCE IN A LIFETIME CHICKEN.

Someone told me you can cook with Coca-Cola. I assume you use it for
basting or for a sauce to cook with. I'm not sure how it would taste since I
haven't personally tried it.

Yet.

The bottom line is not to be intimidated by cooking or by food. Don't eat out
as often. Roll up your sleeves and get your hands in that food and make a
meal so memorable your wife and children will tell all their friends.

And, maybe, just maybe, they'll say something positive, too.

PRETEND FRIED CHICKEN

or

You Can't Fry Anything Without a Deep Fryer

This is your homemade answer to Shake & Bake. Dump some flour in a bowl and add whichever dry seasonings you've been dying to cook with. Make it hot or make it bland. Don't forget dry mustard and crushed fennel seeds. Sage is always nice, and curry adds flavor to anything while being linked to decreased risk of dementia and inflammation.

And if you really want to be experimental, add some cocoa and call it CHOCOLATE CHICKEN.

After you add varying amounts of all kinds of dry seasonings, mix them all together. Either roll each piece of chicken in the mixture, or toss them together in a plastic bag, a piece or two at a time.

Dip in egg or milk if desired before rolling in the dry ingredients. This gives the chicken a thicker batter.

Place the battered chicken pieces on a broiler pan and bake at 350 to 400 degrees for about an hour or so, or until done. If you used smaller pieces, such as breast meat that is cut and bagged, cook for less time.

Try the same thing with other meats, especially pork chops or fish. If you don't have an unusually good memory, or if you don't write down ingredients, you will find that this is also a once in a lifetime experience.

Don't be afraid of a stove. Men tend to be more comfortable with a grill or a campfire and are sometimes intimidated by a stove. Start with an over, broiling or baking, then literally work your way up to the stovetop and a pot.

Remember, throughout history, the greatest chefs have often been men--big, hairy men with deep voices and manly mannerisms. It does not diminish your manhood to boil water.

Just don't forget to turn off the stove.

VEGETABLES

or

I Can't Just Feed Her Meat

Keep bags of frozen vegetables on hand at all times. These can be prepared in only minutes. Potatoes can be baked quickly in the microwave, although their texture will be slightly different. Don't forget baked sweet potatoes. They're one of the most nutritious of all vegetables.

Keep your cupboard stocked with canned vegetables, too. They're not as tasty, but you've probably eaten them in restaurants on occasion without knowing.

You can always add Worcestershire or soy sauce to either frozen or canned vegetables. Experiment with spices and herbs, either fresh or dried. If it doesn't taste good, save it and make soup later.

Cut up some potatoes in small pieces and put them in a pot and cover with water. Add curry powder and call them CURRIED POTATOES. Either boil or cook slowly until done.

Cut up some carrots and toss in a pot with enough water to cover. Toss in a can of bamboo shoots. Add a couple of spoonfuls of honey. Cook until the carrots are soft. Call it CARROTS AND BAMBOO SHOOTS. Or call it BAMBOO SHOOTS AND CARROTS. Or name it for yourself.

Love french fries, but hate the grease? Make oven fries instead. Cut potatoes into pieces, either fat or thin, depending on your preference. Spray some cooking spray on a baking sheet, and spread out the potato pieces. You may choose to spray the potatoes themselves with cooking spray, or you may not.

Bake at 350 until the potatoes are done, probably about an hour. If you want, season before you bake with salt, pepper, or anything else that meets your fancy. You will need to turn them a couple of times while they're cooking. A spatula works well for this. (If you're cooking chicken or something that takes a similar amount of time, then put both in the oven together, being careful to put the potatoes on the top rack.

You can also make a microwave version of oven fries. Simply cut them appropriately (my kids love them cut with a curly cutter someone gave us) and bake until done in the microwave oven.

Nothing in the pantry but a can of pork and beans? Don't despair. Just add a little of this and that and you can create baked beans. Try molasses, barbeque sauce, mustard, soy sauce, and lots of spices of your choice. When in doubt, add spices.

Remember that steamed fresh vegetables are healthier and lower in calories and can add a clean, fresh taste to an otherwise overly seasoned meal. If you don't have a vegetable steamer, or can't figure out how to make one, cook them in just a small amount of water until crispy/soft, whatever that is.

Remember that presentation is half of a good meal. Clean all the clutter off the table and put a flower in a bud vase. If the only flowers you have lack stems, then float them in some water in a pretty bowl. Make sure the flatware, or silverware, or chopsticks, are clean and that there are no hairs on the plates. Turn on some soft music and light a candle or two. Send the kids to bed early and pretend you're on your honeymoon.

And be sure to take a bath and shave before she gets home.

SPAGHETTI

or

You Can Hide Most Anything In There

If you didn't use it in the ONCE IN A LIFETIME CHICKEN, then you can probably put it in the spaghetti sauce. Tomato sauce is a wonder for disguising nearly anything.

I used to add Brussels sprouts to my spaghetti sauce. They sort of resembled meat balls. My wife liked them much better than the time I added sardines, which, by the way, are exceedingly healthful but not recommended in spaghetti sauce.

Don't waste money on overpriced spaghetti sauce when it's so easy to make your own. And don't be intimidated by old wives' tales of it simmering for hours. Mix everything up, add extra seasoning since there isn't time for nuances of flavor to develop, and then put your pot of water on to boil for the noodles. While the leftover sauce will probably get better by the next day, it's quite acceptable to just mix it, cook it a while, and eat it.

Begin with either tomato sauce or tomato paste and water. Don't make it too watery if you like your sauce thick. Chop up an onion and a clove of garlic, or add some dried onion powder and garlic powder. Remember, this is Italian, so add Italian seasonings, such as oregano, sage, rosemary, and thyme. Don't forget bay leaves. If you want to add sweetness, a dash of honey is a good choice. A less good choice is a little ketchup or sugar. Just don't overdo the sweeteners. After all, this isn't a dessert.

Grate a carrot and add it. This will also add sweetness, texture, and vitamins. If you like it hot, add red pepper. Don't forget black pepper and, if you like it and feel adventurous, a little fennel and/or cumin.

You may think this is starting to sound like that chicken recipe, so if you recently cooked that, then make this one different by adding or subtracting either amounts or ingredients. Be creative and have fun.

After all, you're a cook, not a martyr.

If you're like me, you like meat in your spaghetti sauce, even if you know that ground beef is full of fat, various carcinogens, and possibly toxic bacteria. If you want to add ground beef, just brown it first, drain as thoroughly as possible, and add to the sauce. If you really want your cheap ground beef to masquerade as extra lean ground beef, then turn on the hot water facet and rinse the cooked meat a few times, draining into a bowl after each rinse. They even make gadgets to help with this, but the lid of a pot will work if nothing else is available. You may find it easiest to brown the meat first, and then add the tomato sauce and other ingredients.

If you want meatballs instead, or in addition to, make them (they're not hard to make), cook them, and add them to your sauce.

You can substitute ground turkey, which isn't always that much lower in fat since they also grind up the turkey skin, or small pieces of chicken. I don't recommend sardines, but if you especially like sardines, then give it a try.

There are numerous vegetarian versions of ground beef on the market, some in the freezer section and some that are dehydrated, such as textured vegetable protein (TVP), which is made from soybeans. It's dehydrated and saves forever and is always on hand when you're in a hurry or forgot to shop that week. It's best in saucy things, such as spaghetti, burritos, tacos, even lasagna. If you add a little soy sauce or steak sauce, it resembles beef even more.

Beware, however, that there are numerous brands of TVP, and all are not created equal. You will probably have to go to your local health food store to find it, and don't give up if you don't like it initially. Try another brand, and use it a few more times before you pass judgment.

I personally use whole wheat noodles, although some people claim not to like them. I think they're superior, having a pleasant, almost nutty flavor, and much better texture than those bland and mushy white-flour noodles. If you've never had them, you may have to eat them several times to get used to the differences, but if you switch for six months, you'll probably never want to revert back. Whole grains have more fiber, and, if you're like most Americans, you need a whole lot more fiber.

Besides, she'll be so busy trying to figure out what you put in the sauce that she won't notice slightly darker noodles under that tomato sauce covered Brussels sprouts.

CHOCOLATE

or

Remember When They Wouldn't Even Sell
It In Health Food Stores?

As a life-long chocoholic who ate dark chocolate when the only place you could get it was in Belgium, dark chocolate has now become one of the stars of healthy eating. To me, this like finding out that all those mismatched socks in that bottom drawer are really made out of platinum.

Throughout my youth I was faced with carob and sickeningly sweet milk chocolate, searching far and wide for decent bittersweet chocolate.

I remember when carob was touted as a healthy substitute for the supposedly unhealthy chocolate, and health food stores didn't even stock real chocolate.

My, but the times have changed. Carob, which tastes about as much like chocolate as powdered aspirin does, only resembles chocolate in color. I actually saw a poster in a doctor's office recently that listed the ten supposedly healthiest foods, and, lo and behold, there was dark chocolate, right up there with spinach and broccoli.
To use a cliché, who knew?

Carob has gone wherever other food fads go, and health food stores now have whole sections devoted to dark chocolate. Milk chocolate is still taboo, and supposedly for legit reasons, but, as far as I'm concerned, milk chocolate can go the way of carob. To me, it tastes like chocolate-flavored sugar dipped in milk.

While chocolate, even healthy dark chocolate (words I thought I'd never type when I originally wrote this book), is somewhat high in calories, it's still a good substitute for less healthy desserts when that sweet tooth strikes. Just keep a few bars on hand, and break off a piece or two as needed to maintain health.

Think of it as medicine.

AFTERWORD

On the Other Side

My children are no longer children, and the days of diapers and temper tantrums have gone the way of carob. I made mistakes, they made mistakes. I did some things right, they did many things right. I can't imagine life without them, and I don't regret one moment of the time I spent taking care of them when they were young. It wasn't easy all the time, but what worth doing ever is?

Yes, I would do things differently if I could turn back time. I would emphasize family meals, with everyone sitting around the table talking about their day. I would try harder to give them an appreciation of cleaning their rooms and helping with chores. I would rethink the possibility of paying them for chores instead of automatically giving an allowance, an idea I opposed when they were young.

I'm not sure if I would be stricter or less strict. I'm not sure if I would spank or not. I'm not sure if I would be more vigilant as to what they watched on television, but I would definitely pay attention to what they saw on the internet, a problem I didn't have to deal with way back when.
I would stress spiritual matters more, possibly by setting a better example. I would watch even closer who they had as friends, and I would emphasize exercise and fitness more. While we did this on a limited basis, I would encourage family exercise, especially walking. Walking is an exercise they can do long after they're given up soccer and basketball.

I would try to incorporate these things into fun activities done as a family, and I would begin at a very young age when they still want to do the things they are too young to do well. If you can get them to believe that cleaning their bedrooms is fun, then you have changed the world.

Had I done all these things, then my children would today be perfect human beings, flawless, highest-achieving, happy, healthy, and absolute pinnacles of perfection. How could they be otherwise after such perfect upbringing?

What, you don't know anyone like that?

When my youngest child was starting high school, I started college--again. I already had two degrees, but I went back to college in an entirely new field. My youngest was upset with me at the time, as I also had two part-time jobs, but I did this for both my family and for myself.

It was hard, very hard. But, in the long run, it paid off, both financially and personally. I set a good example for my kids, and I was a bit of a role model for beginning anew at an age when some are retiring. My wife was a part of this journey, as she and I went to school together.

You sacrifice for your children, but you are not a slave to them. You owe them much, and they owe you much. My grandmother used to say that you can't repay your parents for all they did for you, but you pass it on to your children. I think she was very wise in this regard.

I'm much older now and a tiny bit wiser. My kids are almost self-supporting, and my wife and I finally have some time together without worrying about babysitters. I look at this time of life as a time for me again, when I can do things I stopped doing after the children were born. I can also begin new adventures, be it a new job or a new hobby. It's like being young again, only with an older, somewhat less perfect body.

OK, so my younger body wasn't so perfect either. At least I had all my hair.

While age is certainly more than a number, it's really health, not age, that matters. If you still have some semblance of health, go back to school. Get a new job if so inclined. Begin a new career.

Don't ever say, "I'm too old." You may have other obstacles to overcome, but age should not be a deterrent to anything worth doing. When the children are finally grown and gone, you can reclaim some of the time you gave to them and use it to rekindle old dreams or to make new ones.

I prefer to say, "I'm not old. I've just been young for a long, long time."

Letter from Cindy

Or

Leave it to a woman to have the last word...

I have always enjoyed working outside the home, so it was a blessing to be married to a man who enjoying staying at home and working to be the primary caregiver for three children when they were young. Looking back, I would do some things differently. Our children are not perfect, but neither are their mom and dad. But, as a family, we are privileged to share this life together, and I am grateful to God for this...and for my wonderful househusband!

www.ingramcontent.com/pod-product-compliance
Lightning Source LLC
Chambersburg PA
CBHW020723160726
47993CB00006B/2329